Unlocking the Writer
in Every Child

About the author

Susan Elkin is an education journalist, former secondary school English teacher and author of over 30 books. She has worked for many years to promote and develop children's writing at all levels.

Also in this series

Unlocking the Reader in Every Child   *Susan Elkin*
     978 184167 970 9

Unlocking the Poet in Every Child   *David Orme*
     978 184167 969 3

Motivating Reluctant and Struggling Readers   *Stephen Rickard*
     978 184167 975 4

Unlocking the Writer
in Every Child

THE book of practical ideas for supporting writing

Susan Elkin

Ransom

Unlocking the Writer in Every Child
by Susan Elkin

Published by Ransom Publishing Ltd.
Radley House, 8 St. Cross Road, Winchester, Hants. SO23 9HX, UK

www.ransom.co.uk

ISBN   978 184167 971 6

First published in 2011

Photographs and illustrations copyright: cover, p47 - Daniel Laflor; arrows - Olena Stinska; jigsaw, cog, dart - Jamie Farrant; p17 - garysludden; p21 - lumen-digital; p22 - Tatiana Popova; p31 - Vadim Ponomarenko; p41 - Irina Behr; p48 - Jaap2; p52 - Carmen Martínez Banús; p59 - Matthias Weinrich, Clayton Hansen, Rouzes, Artur Moszczak, Joanna Pecha, Andrey Armyagov; p71 - DNY59; p83 - Carmen Martínez Banús; p90 - Jacob Wackerhausen; p105 - Olga Krasavina; p112 - gisele; p123 - Carmen Banús, p131 - Chris Halloran, p134 - amaiminta, Jill Chen, TommL, John Said; p144 - Trout55; p157 - Michael Courtney; p171 - Daniel Laflor; p183 - Chris Schmidt; p187 - Dougall Photography; p202 - Carmen Martínez Banús.

Rotherham MBC	
B54 035 634 2	
Askews & Holts	31-Mar-2021
372.623	£22.50
RTSDS	

The right of Susan Elkin to be identified as the author of this Work has been asserted by her in accordance with sections 77 and 78 of the Copyright, Design and Patents Act 1988.

Contents

4   Writing Non-fiction   105

5   Writing with Digital Tools   131

 Introduction

What do we mean by writing? Is it the ability to jot down a shopping list, or to send a text to tell your loved ones that you won't be back until 6pm?

Or is it the composing of 'great writing' such as *Hamlet* or *David Copperfield* or is it a strongly argued, eloquent newspaper article?

And what about words, sentences, stories, essays, reports (and so on) – written by children of all ages? Or the jottings of people who keep private diaries, write poems for pleasure or who blog just because they want to communicate with others?

> 'Write' – which has no fewer than eighteen definitions in my Collins Dictionary (2003) – is an umbrella term.

'Writing' covers all the above and much more.

Writing is not, of course, the sole province of the Shakespeares, Churchills and Newtons of this world, although before universal compulsory education (introduced in 1870 in Britain) many people could not write even their own name.

There is an official document, for example, 'signed' with a cross by John Shakespeare, father of the playwright, when he was Mayor of Stratford.

In the 16th century it was possible to be both a successful businessman (Shakespeare senior was a glover) and completely illiterate.

Today, everyone has to be able to write, and all children are, of course, required to write things in almost every aspect of the curriculum, throughout their schooling and beyond.

Indeed, there are very few jobs, however menial, which don't require some sort of written work.

Reading and writing are complementary skills. Children learn the mechanics of writing by forming for themselves on paper the squiggles they are learning to decode.

 Among other things, a writer is someone who:

🖋 draws or marks (symbols, words etc.) on a surface, usually paper, with a pen, pencil or other instrument

🖋 describes or records (ideas, experiences, etc.) in writing

🖋 composes a letter

🖋 writes words in joined-up script, as opposed to printed style

🖋 is a composer of books, documents, plays, poems, etc.

... and that's before we start on the meanings of 'write down', 'write in', 'write off', and 'write up'.

Writing can be, and is, developed alongside reading and language development – which I discuss in depth in my book *Unlocking the Reader in Every Child* (Ransom Publishing, 2010). But, because writing requires motor skills and coordination, which reading doesn't, it usually comes more gradually.

Somehow, as part of literacy development, we have to find ways of getting children to write – both in very basic, functional ways (e.g. a shopping list) and creatively.

> **Children need to be able to write in many different registers and for a wide range of purposes.**

These purposes might include:

- ✓ letters
- ✓ emails
- ✓ stories
- ✓ reviews
- ✓ factual accounts, such as writing up the results of a science experiment
- ✓ play scripts
- ✓ poems
- ✓ biographical and autobiographical accounts

- ✓ reports
- ✓ interviews
- ✓ notes
- ✓ blogs
- ✓ articles for school magazines or other publications
- ✓ commentaries on, for example, their own art or design technology work

… and much more.

Many children really want to be able to write because they see adults doing it as part of everyday grown-up life – for practical purposes at least. That is why children will often do 'pretend' writing as part of their play activities. This is something to be encouraged, because it's part of the developing awareness that writing – or print – has meaning.

Children also see adults texting, sending emails or messages on Twitter and other social networking sites, and so on. Versions of these kinds of activities, too, can develop as part of play.

Stories and experiences are, of course, a wonderful source of inspiration for children's imaginative writing.

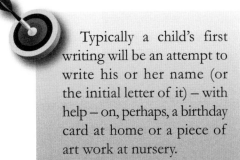

Typically a child's first writing will be an attempt to write his or her name (or the initial letter of it) – with help – on, perhaps, a birthday card at home or a piece of art work at nursery.

Remember, writing is at least three things:

- learning to form (or type) letters, words, sentences and paragraphs

- creating interesting and appropriate blocks of text – generally known as 'good writing'

- expressing ideas in clear, accurate and appropriate language.

Writing is quite hard work. To write at any length, either on paper or using a computer, needs stamina. How do we persuade children to remain interested in it without putting them off for life? This book suggests some solutions.

We also have to work out what we mean by 'good writing'.

Do we mean conventionally correct writing in terms of grammar, punctuation and spelling – known collectively as *orthography*?

Well, obviously these things are very important and must be taught systematically, but they do not in themselves equal 'good' writing.

Fluent, joined-up handwriting matters too, but it isn't the essence of good creative work – which can, of course, be composed just as well on a computer as with a pen on paper. (I am, for example, writing this book using a computer.)

If we want to unlock the writer in every child, we have to teach and develop a wide vocabulary, used in original ways.

Sometimes it is appropriate to break conventional grammar rules (although of course you need to know the rules in order to do that!) or to use punctuation in unorthodox ways. Even spelling is a very different skill from writing well, and can be learned in parallel, separately, and then applied to the child's writing – as we shall see.

Is this book for you?

Many heavily academic books have been written about teaching writing. This is not one of them.

My aim in this book is twofold:

1 to provide a basic, quick-to-read guide to teaching and encouraging writing of all types and at all stages, and

2 to suggest practical 'try this' ideas to help overcome obstacles and, perhaps, to give some fresh perspectives.

So in this book I shall be moving from quick overviews to very 'hands on' things to try with children. That is why each chapter in this book is divided into two parts: first, a quick outline of key issues, followed by a section of practical teaching ideas.

I hope this book will help teachers, special needs co-ordinators, school (and other) librarians and anyone else working in schools, such as learning support assistants, teaching assistants and volunteers who help with literacy work.

But this is not a book just for professionals in schools.

Are you a parent or guardian trying to encourage your children to write? Or are you simply concerned that your children may not be progressing at the rate they should – and in the right way?

If so, you probably need information about how literacy teaching works – in which case this book is for you, too.

We all want to do the best we can to help our children, and developing effective literacy is probably the most important skill they will ever learn.

Remember, though, that no two pupils are the same – and every teacher is different. One size most definitely does not fit all. That is why it's useful to have plenty of strategies for getting reluctant writers going: what works for one pupil in one classroom with a particular teacher or learning assistant won't necessarily work in a different situation.

 So we have to find ways of meeting individual needs. And parents at home, of course, are better placed than anyone to do just that. So don't be afraid to get involved if you want to help your own children.

Let's start with the very youngest ones.

1 Never Too Young to Start

1 Never Too Young to Start

The Issues

 Writing is part of everyday life

Babies are mini learning machines – amongst other things.

Children learn more, and faster, in the first few months after birth than they do at any later stage in their life. This applies as much to their learning the foundations of writing as it does to everything else they learn during this period.

Of course you can't put a pencil in the hand of a new-born baby, but Josh or Emma sees (and hears) adults using pens, pencils, computers, mobile/smart phones and so on from the moment the midwife records the birth weight and the proud dad texts his parents with the good news.

> **W**riting is part of everyday life – from day one.

Babies absorb far more than most adults realise or expect them to. Consider the way young children understand what is said to them (*'It's time for your nap,'* *'Where's your teddy bear?'* and so on) long before they can speak.

> I've never forgotten an experience when I was looking after a young relation aged 10 months for a few hours. Something had upset me, and I stood for a minute looking out of the window, shedding a tear.
>
> Young Jemina crawled across to me and gently stroked my leg to express sympathy. She understood, without being told, that I needed comfort.

The physical activity of writing requires:

✎ **Motor skills**
To make a mark on paper or on a screen, you have to make some sort of muscular movement.

✎ **Co-ordination.**
You have to manage the paper, crayon, screen, keyboard (or whatever you are using) with your hands and your eyes – *and* at the same time.

'Le graphisme'

In France, infants teachers place great emphasis on what they call '*le graphisme*' – a word which doesn't really translate. It means something like 'the graphic act' and involves careful preparation of young children for writing through art work, PE, music and rhythm.

The focus in *le graphisme* is on developing:

✎ overall motor control – the ability to control one's body

✎ fine motor control – the ability to fine-tune the movements of the arm, hand and fingers

✎ visual control of the traces produced by the hand, and

spatial control of one's body, involving awareness of horizontality, verticality and how to transfer a movement onto paper.

Although there is no overall concept of *le graphisme* in the UK education system, it is well worth our bearing the concept in mind as we educate, stimulate and play with young children whose writing skills we hope one day to unlock.

Many of the activities suggested in the second half of this chapter are, effectively, ways of working on *le graphisme*.

Le graphisme has been thoroughly researched by Kent primary school teacher Fiona Thomas, who then applied its principles in her school with very interesting results.

You can read her account of this, 'Une Question de Writing' (1998), at *http://onlinelibrary.wiley.com/doi/10.1111/1467-9604.00054/abstract.*

Early drawing

A child with a crayon is starting to develop the hand control that will eventually be needed to form small letters. That child is also beginning to practise shapes. After all, the 26 letters of the English alphabet are based on circles or part circles, strokes and dots – exactly what the young child draws on the paper.

> Always encourage drawing and art work in the youngest children. It's valuable in itself, but it is also an essential stepping stone on the journey to writing.

Meanwhile you can help the youngest children by playing games with them that use their fingers. Songs with actions, or storytelling in which fingers become puppets and sorting beads, are good examples. Anything that helps strengthen their muscles.

Playing with finger puppets is a great way to develop motor skills.

 ## Shaping letters

As the child's drawing develops, those circles and strokes can gradually be formed into big letters. Usually the first to be formed is the initial letter of the child's name, such as S for Susannah, I for Ishmael, B for Bashar or J for Jasmine. To begin with, they will not be able to write their letters small, lacking the necessary fine motor skills. However the children can colour their big letters in, thus creating illuminated letters for the classroom wall.

> Try to avoid the disjointed 'ball and stick' approach to forming letters. In the past children were often taught that a 'b', for example, is a circle with a straight line next to it or that a 'g' is a circle with a hook underneath.

Instead, encourage the children to shape letters from one continuous, flowing line. Keep the crayon on the paper – which may mean going over some bits of the letter twice. This is important because of a recent development in the teaching of handwriting, which we shall come to shortly.

 ## Progressing to a pen or pencil

If children are very young or very immature they will not be ready to hold a narrow pencil or pen. If you force them before they're ready, they will soon find that writing hurts, because it causes cramp and other problems. That, naturally, puts them off writing – which is the last thing we want.

A s the drawing evolves into writing, and finger skills improve, encourage the child to hold the pencil or crayon with the barrel lying loosely in the angle between the thumb and first finger.

How to hold a pen: the tripod position.

Three basics
for good handwriting

1 **Paper:** use well-spaced, lined paper.

2 **Posture:** make sure that the desk and chair are at the right height. The child should be sitting comfortably, with a straight back.

3 **Pens & pencils:** a sharp HB pencil is recommended to start with. Avoid ballpoint pens.

The first finger should rest bent on the top of the pencil, which is held from the sides by the tip of the thumb and the side of the second finger.

Handwriting experts call this the 'tripod position'. There are special pens and pencils on the market which can help some children with this. These writing implements have a triangular-shaped barrel with shallow concave grooves, so that the children's small digits sit naturally where they should. These pens are in regular use in some schools.

Learning the tripod position – and establishing good habits – will solve many problems later.

 A child who holds a pencil too tightly, or who chooses some other form of grip, will probably have difficulty writing at length. He or she may end up as an adult with problems with repetitive strain injury, too.

If this is not how you hold your own pen or pencil, this might be a good moment to train yourself out of your own bad habits.

Teaching by good example is a teacher's, teaching assistant's or parent's strongest weapon.

 # Handwriting: 'print' or cursive?

Now to that recent development in the teaching of handwriting.

Until about the 1920s all children were taught joined-up – or *cursive* (literally 'running') writing – from the moment they started to write.

Then educationists decided that it would be easier for children if they were first taught to write using separated letters, like the ones they see in printed books.

Then, once that was mastered, the child would be allowed – or encouraged – to join up his or her letters in writing. And for 80 years or so that was how nearly everyone (in the UK at least) learned to write.

Hello, brown cow ...	*Hello, brown cow ...*

'Printed' writing   *Cursive writing*

The problems with this two-stage method are that:

✗   You have to learn to write twice.

✗   The single letters that most children initially were taught to write had no links or hooks (i.e. **they looked like this**). As a result it was difficult for children to adapt to joining up their letters, because they had to learn a new way of forming each letter.

✗ Spaced letters make it hard to distinguish between upper case and lower case letters when the shape is the same, as with s or v, for example:

S s   V v

✗ Many children were not taught how to join up their letters, but rather were left to their own devices. Some children, therefore, went on to write in a laborious, separate-letter style which is very slow.

Since habits once acquired are very hard to break, these children spent the rest of their lives writing in the same, ponderous way.

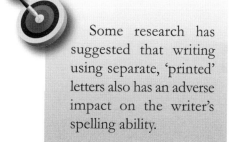

Some research has suggested that writing using separate, 'printed' letters also has an adverse impact on the writer's spelling ability.

✗ Even people who have mastered some form of joined-up writing through this two-stage process often have (or had) very untidy, unattractive, even illegible handwriting in adult life, as a result of letters being badly formed.

One clear advantage of teaching cursive writing from the outset is that it places the focus very much on process.

When a child learns to write using 'printed' letters, the task is to write a letter that 'looks like' the one he or she is trying to copy. This places the focus on the *end result*.

 Teaching writing using the cursive approach also seeks to achieve an acceptable end result (of course), but the joining up of the letters (together with the shape of each letter, with its lead-in and lead-out) focuses more on the *process* of writing – with a good end result being a consequence of following the correct process.

So there is now a move back to teaching children cursive handwriting much earlier. The result seems to be a higher standard of handwriting among nearly all the children in the schools which have adopted this policy. More and more schools are switching to it.

 # Teaching cursive writing from the outset

In addition to the reasons already discussed, teaching cursive writing from the outset brings additional benefits:

- ✓ With cursive writing, words and letters are produced in a flowing movement, which helps the development of a physical memory of how each letter (and word) is written.

- ✓ The smooth, flowing, writing movement makes writing quicker and easier.

- ✓ Letters all start in the same place (with the lead-in) and flow from left to right. This can reduce instances of letter reversal (where *b* is confused with *d*, and *p* with *q*, etc.).

- ✓ Messy transitions, when children move from print to a joined-up style, are avoided.

The biggest disadvantage of teaching children cursive writing is that, from the outset, letters written by the child do not look like the printed letters they find in reading books.

 However, many early reading books use carefully chosen fonts (e.g. from the popular Sassoon family), which offer consistency and which do not depart too far from the way that cursive letters are written.

Incidentally, a cursive style of handwriting is recommended by the British Dyslexia Association.

 # Forming letters

When you are helping children to begin to form letters:

✓ Encourage them to make the letters flowing, one-line creations. One technique which can help is to map a path with dots and then help the child to trace it. (Some cursive computer fonts are commercially available for this purpose, with both complete and 'dotted' versions of the font – sometimes called *trace fonts*.)

Hello, brown cow ...	*Hello, brown cow ...*

Cursive font   *Cursive 'trace' font*

✓ Every letter needs a hook, or lead-in, and a lead-out so that it can be attached to another letter. The hook is part of the flow of the letter. It isn't something added on as an afterthought.

> Every lower case letter should start on the line.

This many not come naturally to you, as you were almost certainly taught 'ball and stick' yourself – so you will have to practise!

There are a number of good books, worksheets and websites which will help you with all this. Try *Handwriting: The Way to Teach It* by Rosemary Sassoon (Sage Publications, ISBN 978-0761943112, 2003 edition). You can find others – there are too many to list – by putting 'cursive writing' into a search engine, or by browsing in a large bookshop. Many of these resources are American in origin, but are equally applicable to the UK.

Left-handedness

About one child in eight is left handed – or to be more accurate, left-dominant. These children will probably walk left foot first and be stronger in the left eye than the right, too.

Keep a particular eye on left-handed children as they learn the mechanics of writing. Encourage them to keep the paper in front of them rather than placing it a long way to one side.

For left-handed children, the paper should be angled about 30 degrees to the left. Help the child to hold the pencil in the same way as their right-handed friends do.

Long gone are the bad old days when adults cruelly forced left-handed children to write with the other hand and regarded left-handedness as sinister.

Incidentally, the word sinister actually comes from *sinistra* – the Latin word for left – which illustrates the old attitude well.

Left-handers are very inclined to devise their own clumsy methods of writing, because they cannot make the conventional ones work for them and they don't always get the right kind of support.

 I have seen left-handed adults, for example, writing by curving the left arm round the top of a piece of paper and angling the hand from the top towards the bottom of the paper – almost writing backwards – so that they can see what they're writing.

Try to stop such habits developing in the very young. You should also make sure that the children have plenty of working space. If a right-handed child sits too close to a left-hander, for example, they will jog each other because their working arms are side by side. That is not, of course, an argument for segregating the left-handers. Just make sure that they are not squashed!

Adults as scribes

Very young children often know what they want to write, but cannot yet write it.

 For example, children might want their daily news recorded or a caption put under a picture for display.

So they need an adult to write it down for them. In education jargon this process is called 'scribing' and the adult who does the writing a 'scribe'.

Listen carefully to what the children say, and write it in a way that can be read by the more advanced readers in the class, family or group, or by visitors from elsewhere (e.g. from another class).

This is all part of showing the children that writing is important and valued by grown ups.

 A single sentence is usually enough. If the child can manage it, he or she could sign what you have written by writing their name at the bottom.

Forming words

Once children can form letters and are beginning to read words (using a phonics-based system), there is almost unlimited scope for writing.

✓ The child's own name should always be the first target – with the given name first. Then work on the family name as soon as the child is comfortable with writing his or her given name. Soon a child should be able to write 'Susan Elkin' or 'Panjit Singh' without too much help.

It's best to avoid the term 'Christian name' in school, because children from non-Christian cultures don't have them. 'First name' is tricky too, because Chinese people, for example, put the chosen name after the family name. 'Given name' seems to fit the bill best.

✓ They will also want to write words like 'Mum', 'Dad', 'Nan' and the names of siblings. Make sure that you know how siblings' and other relations' names are spelled. Many can be spelled more than one way ('Catherine', 'Katherine', 'Kathryn' and 'Catharine', or 'Leigh', 'Lee', 'Lea', etc.).

Names from a culture other than your own are a potential minefield. If you're in any doubt ask the child's parent (or whoever brings the child to school).

Almost any game or activity you can devise which encourages children to put letters together to form words and write them is likely to be useful and to support other work the children are doing.

Let your imagination rip.

Sentence building

Words are the building blocks of sentences. As soon as children can make words, they can begin to put them in order.

In practice, children can start to write sentences as soon as they can write a word or two.

Use the child's own name and start with the simplest phonetic words, so you get sentences like 'Jamila runs' or 'Daniel sits'.

 Get the children to write and illustrate their sentences.

Then you can move on to slightly more complex sentences, such as 'Dad and I went to the swimming pool,' or 'Raj has eaten his banana'. You may want to write down some of these first, for the children to copy. Alternatively they can just make them up.

From there it's only a short hop to writing for real.

1 Never Too Young to Start

Practical Teaching Ideas

Finger painting

Making marks on paper is the very beginning of writing, and it is never too soon to start.

In France this would be part of *le graphisme*.

✐ This activity shows children that they can use their fingers and paint to make marks. They can then look at their work and share it with others. Doing this with an adult 'legitimises' this aspect of play, especially when their work receives praise and they are positively encouraged.

✐ You need:

* wet, easily washable paint: powder paint mixed with water is ideal. One bright colour will do.

* large sheets of paper – the backs of old rolls of wallpaper work well – so does newspaper.

*   non-toxic sticky tape.

*   a bowl of water and soap, or similar.

If the child is still a baby, dip his or her hand in the paint and help with the making of handprints on the paper. If the child is a toddler, it is easier to strap him or her into a high or low chair with a tray, or at a table. Tape the paper down so that it doesn't slip. Encourage the dipping of fingers into the paint and making patterns on the paper. Most children will use both hands at this stage, and you will see hand prints as well as finger marks and prints.

> Talk about what Ella or Jack is doing, the colour of the paint and what the images might look like (e.g. an animal or a cloud).

Add the child's name to the work. Let him or her see you write it and explain what you're doing. Display the work on the wall.

The children can also use their feet to make prints and marks on paper, in the same way.

Similarly, let the child experiment with a brush, once he or she can hold one.

When the painting is finished, wash the worst of the paint off hands in the nearby bowl. Finish the cleaning job in the bathroom!

Talk about the marks on the paper. Ask the child what he or she has painted. It is a reminder that marks on paper can have meaning – whether they make words or not.

Fly away Peter

Little games like this one help to get the fingers moving ready for later writing – a nod to *le graphisme*. This game helps children develop finger movement and move one finger independently of the others. It gets them chanting in rhythm and making arm movements, too.

✎ All you need is a table or tray edge. You and the children put the tips of your index fingers on the edge of the table.

✎ You chant:

> *Two little song birds sitting on a wall,*
>
> *One named Peter, one named Paul.*
>
> *Fly away Peter*
> (raising left hand into the air before putting it away in your lap)
>
> *Fly away Paul*
> (raising the other hand and putting it away in your lap)
>
> *No little song birds sitting on a wall.*
>
> *Come back Peter*
> (bring left finger back to the table)
>
> *Come back Paul*
> (bring the other finger back)
>
> *Two little song birds sitting on a wall.*

✎ You will probably want to play this several times, until all the children have learned it. In any event, play the game four times using the four fingers in turn. Then encourage each child in the group to do it solo, in turn.

To develop motor skills further, try playing a singing game with slightly more complicated actions, such as:

> *Incy Wincy spider climbed up the spout,*
> (two hands make spider climbing)
>
> *Down came the rain and washed the spider out,*
> (fluttering, descending fingers become rain)
>
> *Out came the sun and dried up all the rain,*
> (arms wide)
>
> *So Incy Wincy spider climbed up the spout again.*
> (as line 1)

 ## Scribing

When an adult records a child's ideas or words before he or she is old enough to do it, this is (as we have seen) called 'scribing'.

Scribing shows that writing is useful. It also demonstrates that children's words are valuable. And it gets them talking. All you need is a large pad and a pen.

- Encourage a very young child to tell you some news, such as 'Mum and I went to the shop and got my new shoes,' or 'It's my brother's birthday today.' A slightly older child may be able to tell you more elaborate news – such as 'We had fish for tea. Mum got it at the shop because my uncle Adam was coming. He likes fish and so do I.'

- Or coax out a made-up story. 'Once upon a time there was a princess. She was really scared because she heard a big noise in the night. But when her mum went to look it was just the dog knocking some plates over in the kitchen ... .'

- Write the news or story as clearly as you can and in quite large letters on your pad.

- Always add the child's name (or get him or her to do it) and make a wall display of the work.

> Try to extend the child's work by asking questions, so that more sentences are added.

> Get two children to make up a story together. Then you could move on to a group story – each child in a circle adds a bit to the story while you scribe it.

Pretend writing

Before they can write, children love to pretend that the lines they make on paper are writing. This is to be encouraged, because it reinforces the concept that lines on paper have meaning.

It also develops the motor skills needed for writing and teaches 'writing behaviour'.

- All you need is paper and pencils, felt tips or fine crayons.

- Ask the children to 'write' – letters, stories, shopping lists or anything you or they can think of. Make it clear that this is a 'let's pretend' game.

> As the children get better at this game, encourage the older or more adept ones to make their writing more like 'real' writing by making lines across the page from left to right.

When they have put some marks on their paper get them to 'read' each other's writing. Start this off yourself.

Say '*What is it, Lily?*' If she tells you it's a shopping list, you can then pretend to read what's on it. '*Oh yes, I see you're going to buy some apples, a packet of pasta and a tube of toothpaste, Lily.*'

Or if Henry tells you his is a story, you pretend to read it aloud. Once the other children see what you're doing, they will copy by 'reading' each other's work too.

Writing your name

As we have seen, most children learn to write their names before they write anything else.

 Concentrate on the initial letter of each child's name to start with. Then fill in the rest of the name, using an upper case (or 'capital') letter to start, followed by lower case ('small') letters. At first, make the letters very large so that they almost fill the paper. As the children become more skilled with a pencil, the letters will get smaller. Big shapes are much easier for small hands to manage.

 Gradually build up the number of letters the child can manage. Bear in mind that it can be a real effort for a young child to remember the order in which they come, particularly if it's a long name.

> Children with simpler names (e.g. Tom or Raj) will almost certainly learn to write their names more quickly and easily than a Charlotte or Nicholas.

Filling in gaps

Write words with gaps in them, such as *d__g, h__n, shar__, __us, ja__*, etc. Present the words with pictures of the objects alongside and ask the children to fill in the spaces with letters.

> You can very easily devise worksheets along these lines using clipart, pictures from magazines or copyright-free images from the Internet. Alternatively, if you prefer, you could draw your own.

Spelling practice

Give the children three or four words to write across the top of a sheet of paper (or do it for them). For example: *park, nest, match* and *pink*. Then ask them to list as many words as they can, by changing the first letter of each word. So you might get:

> *park, dark, bark, mark ...*
> *nest, best, pest, rest ...*
> *match, latch, hatch ...*
> *drink, link, think ...*

and so on.

Then they can decorate the edges of the paper. This helps with spelling – but don't tell the children that. Just let them have fun with the creativity of it.

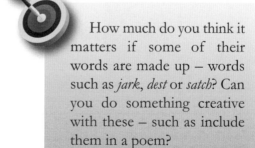

How much do you think it matters if some of their words are made up – words such as *jark, dest* or *satch*? Can you do something creative with these – such as include them in a poem?

 # Word building

✍ Give the children some word openings, such as *thr__*, *gr__*, *qu__*, and *bl__*. Ask them to list as many words as they can using each of these openings, such as:

throw, three, throne ...
growl, grab, grey ...
quick, queen, quiz ...
blue, blood, black ...

The children will probably enjoy decorating the rest of the paper to finish the job.

You can also do this activity with word endings, such as *__ing, __end, __ake*, etc., so that you might make:

sing, ring, king ...
bend, friend, lend ...
cake, make, quake ...

Almost any game or activity you can devise which encourages the children to put letters together to form words is likely to build their literacy skills.

 # Story characters you know

Characters from familiar stories are a good subject to write about. This is also a good way of linking reading with writing.

✍ Ask the children to think of a person or animal they know from a familiar story (e.g. *Cinderella*, *Mog* or *The Gruffalo*). Help the children to write the character's name on the paper.

Depending on each child's ability and developmental stage, you might:

- write it for the child to copy
- let him or her write the first letter and you write the rest

- • trace the letters that you have first outlined
- • let the child write it with your spelling help
- • let the child write it unaided
- • let the child copy it from the book.

 Once the name is on the paper the children can draw a picture to go with it. Children who are ready to move on could also write a simple sentence about the character.

 # Writing and sending letters

Sending pretend (or real) letters is fun, and teaches children a lot.

 Encourage the youngest children to make a game of 'writing' and/or drawing on a sheet of paper, then putting it an envelope and giving it to someone else – saying *'Here's a letter for you.'*

 You could even develop this into a 'let's pretend' game, in which one child takes the role of the postman and another is someone at their front door. (This might be a good opportunity to look at Janet and Allan Ahlberg's book *The Jolly Postman.*)

> Any adult being given such a letter should, of course, make a point of opening and 'reading' it with appropriate comments. Older children can probably write at least their name on the paper, together with the name of the person the letter is for.

 # Making notices, labels and signs

If you want notices, labels and signs in the classroom (or at home), don't make them all yourself. Get the children to help you.

Large crayons are ideal at the early stages of 'writing'.

Help beginner writers to make a notice by tracing the letters lightly on a card. Use lower case letters except the first, which should be upper case. Then help the children to trace over them with a marker pen or crayon. As the children become more practised, they may be able to do it by copying from a separate paper rather than using the guide lines. Make notices which say, for example:

Our book corner
Nature table
Dressing up box
Sand and water.

As they get more practised, encourage the children to produce labels, notices and signs more independently. Some might soon even be able to make printed signs using a computer: more on this in Chapter 5, *Writing with Digital Tools*, page 131.

You can also make labels for displays of children's work and anything else which is going on in the room.

Writing news

Daily news writing is a classic but enjoyable and worthwhile early years activity. Children share news with each other informally all the time. Or they single out adults to whom to tell things like '*My dad's got a new car,*' or '*My hamster's had babies.*' Circle time promotes news sharing too.

   Get the children to write some of this down each day. With younger children, you may have to scribe it for them (see above). Older children can be helped to write a sentence about the news themselves. Start by getting the child to work out what he or she wants to write.

With less advanced children, write the sentence but leave one word for the child to fill in. As they get better at this, more of them will be able to write a whole sentence (or more) with help.

> Once the news is written you can display it on the wall, keep it in a personal folder (one for each child so that it builds up to a day-by-day diary) or send it home with the child at the end of the day.

Children can gradually begin to write at greater length and/or to use a computer as an alternative to handwriting.

Writing rhymes

Most children love playing with words, and it's fun to write down some of the results.

Ask the children to think of some boys' and girls' names to pair with rhyming adjectives. For example:
Silly Sally
Thirsty Kirsty

Jolly Ollie
Tall Paul
Hairy Mary.

> Look at rhyme books with the children – such as *Bobbie Shafto Clap your Hands* (A&C Black) or *Chanting Rhymes* by John Foster and Carol Thompson (OUP). It will give you and them more ideas for your own rhymes.

✎ Then help the children to write down the ones they've thought of. Even quite young children are often good at thinking of rhyming words, although it may be the older ones who do most of the writing. Some children may want to extend the rhyme by adding more:

Jolly Ollie bought a lolly for his sisters, Molly and Polly.
Tall Paul saw the ball fall.

Writing lists

The writing of lists is grown-up behaviour which children like to imitate.

✎ The activity is best approached as a shopping activity. Say: '*Let's play shops. Now Mrs Jones, have you got your list? What's on it today?*' Or pretend to be looking at a list and collecting things from the shelf in the supermarket.

✎ In this way you can build the making of marks on a piece of paper – your shopping list – into 'let's pretend' games about shopping with the children.

✎ For older or more advanced children, help them to make a real list. Talk about what to put on it. List several items and then use the list as the basis of the shopping game – ideally in several different shops. The memory game '*I went to the shop and I bought*

...' can be adapted with a group. They can each try to write down the items as they are mentioned, to remind them of the list.

 Most children are happy to list anything. Try activities like '*Let's see how many animals/ birds/ flowers/ colours we can think of and write them in a list.*'
  Or you could:

- ask them to list everything they have to bring to the school or centre from home each morning ('*so that we don't forget anything!*')
- ask them to list everything they are wearing
- put five or six random articles on a tray for the children to list.

 ## Let's make a story

As the children gradually master composing and/or writing skills, encourage them to try making stories like the ones they are used to hearing.

There are three levels at which you can do this activity, depending on the developmental stage of the children:

- Get the children to tell their stories and scribe their writing for them.
- Encourage them to write single words in sentences that you write.
- If they can, help them to write the sentences themselves.

The conversation might go something like this:

You: What is the story about?
Child: Robert, and he's five.

> *You:* So shall we write 'There was once a boy called Robert who was five'?
>
> *Child:* Yes, and can we say he lives in a big house near a wood? ...

And so on.

 Once the story is finished, the writer can illustrate it. You can build a story of this sort by working with a single child, or make it a communal story put together by a group.

> Each time you do this activity, aim to make the story a little more complex than the time before – more sentences, more going on in the story and more detail.
>
> Get the children to read their stories aloud to each other. Video them, so they can see themselves telling the story – and show it to members of their families.

2 Persuading Children to Write

2 Persuading Children to Write

The Issues

Reading and writing

Literacy is a two-sided coin: it has reading on one side and writing on the other. The two skills are more than complementary. They depend on each other.

Writing develops from reading. A child cannot write anything unless he or she can also read it.

So we have to teach and develop writing alongside reading. My parallel book to this one (*Unlocking the Reader in Every Child*, Ransom 2010) focuses on developing reading – but bear in mind that we can never totally separate the one skill from the other.

To an extent reading is enhanced by writing too. Children and young people can be encouraged, for example, to read each other's writing. They can also be 'turned on' to both reading and writing by meeting and working with published authors (see Chapter 6, *Working with Professional Writers*, page 157).

> Once children have mastered the rudiments of writing individual words, we can focus on ways of helping them to write imaginatively, creatively, incisively – and, ultimately, with technical accuracy.

Stories

Teachers typically ask children to invent and write stories. Although some of the results may be lacklustre and very brief, most children in Key Stage 1 or early in Key Stage 2 in UK schools (that's ages approx. 6 – 11) are willing to have a go, even if they still need a lot of help with the mechanics.

They're willing to 'have a go' because they have been exposed to plenty of fiction in school, if not also at home. They understand narratives and they know how stories work. These children are also usually too young to have developed negative feelings about their abilities, and their imaginations are fresh and uncluttered.

> Although it may seem obvious, never forget that adults need to share as many stories as possible with children for their imaginations to develop.

The stories can be about (almost) anything: fairy tales, folk stories, sport, dinosaurs, families, issues (such as family break-up), ghosts, fantasies, science fiction, story poems and so on. Even the best non-fiction books are often written as narratives (e.g. the 'story' of the space race, or the discovery of America).

 Aim for maximum variety in what you offer, because (of course) different children are drawn to different things.

Children who are steeped in stories are more likely to want to make up stories of their own than children who lack exposure to fiction. Share stories – as stimuli for writing – by:

✓   reading aloud

✓   sharing a picture book, but improvising the story

✓   telling (without a text)

✓   encouraging children to tell stories to each other

✓   bringing a professional storyteller into school.

Then move on to spin off ideas from the shared stories which the children might develop.

Creative writing and creative reading

When a child (or adult) reads, inevitably he or she uses imagination. The writer writes and the reader reads. Both reader and writer are creating images in their heads – although the images in each case are not necessarily the same.

In school we try to develop children as imaginative readers to the highest possible level. We also aim to develop the creativity of their writing. The two are closely connected.

Reading connects with writing because it:

✓   provides ideas for the reader's own writing

✓   teaches new words

✓   shows the many ways in which words can be used to create interesting sentences, and

✓ can provide the facts needed for a piece of writing (e.g. the date of an invention, or the colours of the rainbow – both of which could be found in a reference book or on the Internet).

A child's writing, meanwhile:

✓ provides something for another creative reader to read

✓ shows clearly what the child has read, or likes to read, and

✓ can be a way of communicating the pleasure of reading to someone else – in a book review, for example.

 So be very aware of the importance of reading and books when you are encouraging children to write and/or helping them with their writing.

Declining interest in fiction

As they progress through primary school, some children's reading and writing skills will plateau, or even decline. There are a number of possible reasons for this.

✗ Reading ability can easily stop improving because once the mechanics of reading have been taught, too many teachers neglect the development of sustained, fluent reading.

✗ Writing immediately becomes less imaginative if the writer is not experiencing stories regularly.

✗ Without the ability to read quickly, effortlessly and independently for meaning, it is impossible to write fluently.

✗ A child who cannot write fluently (particularly when some other class members can) will likely develop a negative 'can't do it' attitude and stop trying.

✗ He (and it is often, but not invariably, a boy) will tend to gravitate towards finding ways of avoiding writing as much as possible.

 This can mean a further decline in writing ability, creating a downward spiral.

✗ Some children, especially boys, lose interest in 'sissy' or 'uncool' stories very early, as other interests such as football or computer games take over.

Don't underestimate computer games.

Don't underestimate computer games. Many such games are, in fact, fiction narratives, although young players won't usually see them as such.

> We all need to accept that fiction in books isn't the be-all and end-all of children's reading and writing.

That means we must encourage (or allow) children to read more widely and we must respect all genres of reading as much as fiction.

All writing has the same aim: to communicate ideas, thoughts and feelings, or to convey a message.

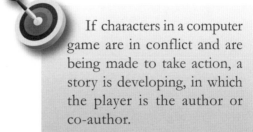

If characters in a computer game are in conflict and are being made to take action, a story is developing, in which the player is the author or co-author.

 The most effective writing is:

- **clear** – the reader can understand it

- **concise** – enough words to ensure that the message is understandable, but not so many as to obscure the meaning

- **exact** – it uses appropriate, accurate vocabulary and follows spelling, punctuation and grammar conventions

- **appropriate** – it adopts the right tone for the situation and the reader.

Writing for 'real' purposes

Instead of merely practising with letters, words and contrived sentences (*'Time for our writing lesson,'* – what a turn off!), you can instead encourage children of all ages to write for real purposes.

These purposes might include:

- ✓ news
- ✓ blogs
- ✓ wikis
- ✓ stories
- ✓ letters
- ✓ emails
- ✓ (for older children) Facebook posts or 'tweets' on Twitter
- ✓ poems
- ✓ postcards
- ✓ diaries
- ✓ greetings cards
- ✓ articles for the school magazine or website
- ✓ notices for the classrooms
- ✓ shopping lists
- ✓ instructions
- ✓ plays
- ✓ recipes
- ✓ notes
- ✓ factual accounts
- ✓ record of findings or observations

… and many other forms of writing.

Many of the above (which is by no means an exhaustive list, by the way) can be either handwritten or produced electronically.

So how much should we encourage the use of computers and digital media when we're trying to unlock the writer in every child? We'll discuss this further in Chapter 5, *Writing with Digital Tools*, page 131.

Consider e-post and greetings cards, for example. A blog is really only an electronic diary, and things such as recipes can be presented in any format you like.

When children are writing, be prepared to:

- offer the occasional idea for a story which gets 'stuck'

- suggest a rhyme for a poem

- advise children where they can get information

- help with ICT if a computer is being used, and/or

- read through written work which is finished or under way, and provide feedback.

Above all be flexible. Accept that there are almost as many approaches to writing as there are children. There is no single method of unlocking young writers. There's a cupboard full of keys – and you need access to as many of them as possible.

2 Persuading Children to Write

Practical Teaching Ideas

Frameworks for writing

In literacy teaching the word 'framework' refers to a structure, around which children can write. Usually a framework is a diagram with boxes for the children to write in. These boxes are empty, or contain just a few outline words. Each box represents a paragraph and the child has to fill in the boxes.

Many teachers now encourage children to write using a

For many pupils, using a framework is less daunting than sitting down in front of a blank sheet of paper or screen.

So, say, a story might have six paragraphs. In the first someone (the child decides who) goes somewhere (the child decides where) and sees something strange (the child decides what.)

framework to hang their story or other writing on. (Indeed some teachers refer to frameworks as 'scaffolding'.) In effect it means that the basic shape of the written piece is laid out but the child fills the details.

> Frameworks are a useful way of helping a child to shape a piece of writing. The outline supports their ideas – just as scaffolding supports a building.

 There are many published schemes offering frameworks for writing, often with photocopiable resources for the children to use.

One example is *Writing Frameworks: Easy to use structures for creating confident successful writers* by David Whitehead (published by Stenhouse Publishers, 2003).

Or you might devise some frameworks of your own.

✍ Frameworks can be used to do much more than just provide paragraph structures, however. For example, the various components of a story can in themselves constitute a series of frameworks:

- the characters
- the setting
- what happens in the story, and
- how the story ends.

✍ Make a clear distinction between the mechanics of writing – whether writing by hand or typing – and the process of creating an original piece of writing. We tend to use the same word ('writing') for both, which can be confusing.

✍ There might be times, for example, when you want to do a handwriting or typing exercise with a group (or with individuals), because problems have emerged in class. But this is not the same as a creative writing exercise.

W hen you are trying to get children to write imaginatively, informatively or accurately, don't focus on the mechanics of how to form letters. It will distract them from the content of what they're writing.

The aim, of course, is that eventually they will be able to do both at once.

Creative sentences

✏ Give the children a list of words and challenge them to make up the most interesting or funniest sentences they can from them. This is something you can do with children of any age, but if the children are older (or particularly able) make sure that the words are more challenging.

So for a very young or limited group you might give them: *Marie, bat, an, the, held, sat, asked, funny, quickly*, etc.

For a more advanced group you could list: *principal, wondered, reason, energy, mouldering, the, an, lay, personal, it's* – and so on.

✏ The children need not use every word in every sentence.

Building stories around objects

✏ An object is a powerful starting point for a story. You can use any kind of object, whether it be a large shell, an old map, a broken bottle or a football shirt.

Any kind of object can be a starting point for a story.

✏ Begin by showing the object to the children. Encourage discussion: '*Who might be using this map?*' '*A pirate?*' '*Where is he? Where does he want to go?*' Then let the children write a story or a poem of their own devising.

✏ As an alternative, you could work on the story shape as a group (working out the broad shape of the story and identifying the central characters, etc.). Then each child could write his or her own version of the story – with embellishments as they see fit.

✏ Story boxes, story bags or story sacks are usually associated with a pre-chosen story. They contain 'props' (such as a big growly teddy bear, a porridge bowl and spoon for *The Three Bears)* to help tell the story. You can buy commercial story boxes, or make your own.

 Try putting together some objects which are not linked to a specific story. Then encourage the children to create a story around the objects.

Story Cubes® (*www. storycubes.com*) are a variant of story boxes. I discuss these in more detail on page 152.

 You might include, for instance, a football sock, a whistle, a plate and a photograph of a child.
Or a swimming hat, a tube of suncream, a photograph of a shark and an alarm clock.

Describing objects

 Show the children an object – such as a very old newspaper, a large, knobbly potato or a hand-knitted cardigan. Let then touch it, hold it, smell it, hear it rustle (and so on) as well as see it.

 Then ask them to describe the object in writing – as if they were describing it to someone (or something!) from Mars, who has no experience of such an object and doesn't know what it is or what it is for.

 Encourage the children to be concise. They should use as few sentence as possible and be as accurate as possible.

Writing instructions

✐ Set the children the task of writing instructions for an everyday activity, such as making a piece of toast with jam, or sharpening a pencil.

✐ This is good practice at writing clearly and for a purpose. The children will first need to think through the activity logically, step by step. If appropriate, work though the stages with them first.

Anecdotes

✐ Get the children to describe a real life experience in writing. The experience could be something very ordinary, such as the rain on the way to school one morning, or yesterday's school dining queue (this is good for Key Stage 3 children).

✐ The piece of writing need not be very long. The object is to create a lively read.

Anything can be made to seem fascinating if it's told in an entertaining way.

Verses for greetings cards

✐ It's a common class activity in schools for children to make greetings cards for Easter, Christmas, Hannuka, the Chinese New Year, Mothering Sunday, Father's Day and so on. But the emphasis is usually on the art work rather than on writing. This activity focuses on the writing.

Shop-bought greetings cards often contain verses. Collect some examples to read with the children. Then encourage them to try writing their own personalised verse for a specific occasion.

Other occasions you could suggest they write for:
- grandparents' 40th wedding anniversary
- a 'get well' card for a friend in hospital, recovering after a road accident
- congratulations to a family friend who has just passed their driving test
- Diwali good wishes to a neighbour
- a birthday card for a parent
- wishing somebody a happy Jewish New Year.

 # Epitaphs

Despite their connotations of death, epitaphs can be fun and they appeal to many children because they are – or can be – very short.

 Explain to the children that an epitaph is a statement on a gravestone or other memorial. It may express the feelings of the relatives or it may praise, or comment on, the qualities of the dead person.

 An epitaph can be just a few plain words, such as 'Much loved wife, mother and grandmother'. But epitaphs are not always solemn. Some are really quite funny, such as this one from a cemetery in America:

Here lies Lester Moore
Four slugs from a .44
No Les
No more.

✎ Or they can be longer such, as this famous one for Frederick,
Prince of Wales (1707–1751):

> Here lies poor Fred
> Who was alive and is dead.
> Had it been his father,
> I had much rather;
> Had it been his brother
> Still better than another;
> Had it been his sister
> No one would have missed her;
> Had it been the whole generation
> So much better for the nation;
> But since 'tis only Fred
> Who was alive and is dead,
> Why, there's no more to be said.

✎ Read some epitaphs with the children. A quick search on the
Internet will find you plenty of sites listing them, but not all are
suitable for (younger) children. So it's best that you select some
epitaphs to print out, rather than directing the children to the
sites.

✎ Once they've got the idea of writing epitaphs, encourage the
children to write an epitaph for a sporting or show business
hero, or for someone known to them.

 ## Using books as a starting point

Books that children have read can be a great starting point for writing
activities. Consider, for example, getting children of any age (once they can
read) to do any of the following.

✎ To write a poem modelled on one they've read.

- To write a short account of facts they have learned from a book they have read – for example, (after reading Sally Gardner's *I Coriander*) what happened to the people who supported the king in mid-17th century England. Or (after reading *The White Giraffe* by Lauren St John) what happened to the animals of South Africa. Almost any fiction book has some factual background.

- To note down six new words learned from, say, a Harry Potter book.

- To email a friend to tell him or her about a book the writer has enjoyed.

- To write a letter or postcard, perhaps to a grandparent, commenting on a book.

- To keep a list of books read – i.e. a reading log, with titles accurately written. The list should include publisher, author and other details.

 This is a good habit for young readers to get in to. It means they can easily find books they've read in the past when they want to look at them again. And it helps teach them to value reading.

- To write sequels and other additions to books they've read. This could include an additional chapter, or a new story involving one of the characters.

- To make notes based on non-fiction books.

- To write to the author of any book they have enjoyed, congratulating or thanking him or her and perhaps asking some polite questions. Most authors will answer letters from children, which is very exciting for the letter writer. (Authors can always be contacted by writing to them c/o their publisher.)

Following up film and TV

If a child has seen and enjoyed a film, encourage him or her to look on the Internet (with appropriate supervision) to find some online reviews. Read them together – either with an adult or in a pairing with another child who has seen the same film.

- Once you have done this a few times – and after perhaps being gently nudged into looking at film reviews in other media, such as magazines or newspapers – the child will have some idea of what reviews look and feel like.

- You might then suggest that after the next film Max or Lizzie write his or her own review, before going on to read reviews by others.

- Find some way of 'publishing' the child's review – e.g. on a noticeboard, in a class portfolio for others to read, or on the school intranet. Or email it to friends, or (if the children are old enough) put it on Facebook.

Publishing a child's work gives it a legitimacy it would not otherwise have. This is extremely empowering for the child. His or her writing is being taken seriously.

Here's another example: if a child is very excited (obsessed?) by, say, a football hero, then introduce the art of writing a mini biography.

- First help the child to do some research – to double check things such as dates, what the player did before playing for his (or her) current club,

And if Lizzie or Max doesn't feel up to writing at length, consider publishing a review on Twitter (of which more later).

Because Twitter allows only 140 characters per entry, it is quite a discipline to say something worthwhile very succinctly – and it's definitely good writing practice.

what they have achieved and a bit about other activities they might be involved in (e.g. charity work).

 This can be shaped into a very informative six sentence or so mini-biography.

> You can, of course, do the same thing with anyone in the public eye: film stars, pop singers, TV personalities, politicians – even authors.

Activities for children who are struggling

Some children find writing particularly difficult. This might be because they have a particular type of special educational needs (e.g. dyslexia), or English might be their second (or additional) language (ESL or EAL).

Whatever the reason, the following activities focus on supporting these children in their writing.

Supporting struggling children aged 5 – 6 (UK Key Stage 1)

 Include games and activities which involve moving the fingers in finely controlled ways – such as using Lego or using the fingers for action in rhymes.

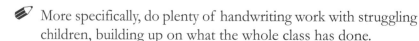

Almost all children who need extra help with writing also need help to improve 'motor skills' or controlled body movement. Remember 'le graphisme'.

 More specifically, do plenty of handwriting work with struggling children, building up on what the whole class has done.

✏ If the child is ready, help him or her to write his or her name, together with some simple words. But don't force it.

✏ Show the children some pictures collected from magazines or using the Internet. Talk about what the children can see in the pictures, and get them to write down what they can see.

> You could extend this activity by asking the children to write down what they might hear, as well (e.g. for a woodland scene – birds singing, trees rustling).

✏ If necessary, 'scribe' what each child would like to write and show him or her word by word what you have written.

Remember that a child suffering from attention deficiency or hyperactivity (whatever the cause) will achieve more if presented with many small tasks rather than one big one.

Supporting struggling children aged 7 – 11 (UK Key Stage 2)

From the age of around seven, dyslexia and similar problems may be coming apparent in some children. Dyslexia can be diagnosed in younger children, but quite often (too often?) it isn't fully recognised until a child is eight or nine at the earliest.

✏ For all children at this age who are struggling with writing, you will need to provide continued support to help them develop their skills.

✏ As ever, read to these children as much as you can. The more language they hear, the more likely they are to catch up – and that particularly applies, obviously, to pupils learning English as a second language.

✏ If you have even two minutes left at the end of a session after packing up, read aloud a poem, a joke, a paragraph from a newspaper, the opening passage from an exciting book, or a short piece from a reference book which has caught your eye.

✏ Have some hand-writing practice worksheets to hand. Some children will need continued help with handwriting, as well as needing help with what to write.

Encourage the children, if they can, to write about what they have heard or read. Many of the strugglers are likely to be behind with their own reading, so they may be short of writing ideas.

⚙ Supporting struggling children aged 11 – 14 (UK Key Stage 3)

Different problems can begin to emerge in older children. First, any child who still needs help with writing is probably quite demoralised. Behaviour problems are quite likely to go with that, too.

Second, because the secondary school curriculum is usually subject-based, there will be a wide range of writing tasks relating to different subjects. (This applies equally to schools outside the UK as well.)

Help with writing can give a child over eleven access to the wider curriculum.

The aim, of course, is to give these children the same access to learning that the rest of the class has – and that necessarily includes helping them to write things down.

These children will probably need:
- help with spelling
- suggestions for words
- help with filling in charts and grids with written words
- to be shown where they can find what they need to write down (whether it be in a text book, on the whiteboard or elsewhere).

And, of course (as always), they will need lots of praise to build self esteem.

3 Fiction, Plays and Poems

3 Fiction, Plays and Poems

 The Issues

Having discussed fiction briefly in Chapter 2 and acknowledged that, sadly, it doesn't turn all children on, let's look at some ideas for unlocking writers who do want to write stories in some form. Then in the next chapter we'll turn to non-fiction writing.

The scope of fiction

The first thing to accept about fiction, I think, is that it's a great deal wider than the '*he said, she said*' narratives of novels and stories.
   Fiction includes:

   ✓ comic strips with captions

   ✓ play scripts

   ✓ poems (although not all poetry can really be considered as fiction)

✓ made-up diaries

✓ made-up letters/emails/Facebook posts etc., which tell some sort of story.

And that's before you start on the forms of fiction which don't involve reading – such as TV soaps, wordless strip cartoons, oral jokes, films, plays (when seen or heard but not read as a script), oral storytelling, the 'make believe' play of very young children, and so on.

Some psychologists argue that every human being has a deep need for fiction. Without it we can't work things out in real life. It's almost as basic as food, drink and air.

All major religions are supported by a body of stories. In the Bible, for example, people live, love, fight, talk, give birth, do heroic deeds, travel, die and so on. Many of the stories in the Old Testament, (sometimes known as the Hebrew Bible) are shared by Jews and Muslims. Indian religions, such as Hinduism, have many stories too.

Is this another example of the human need for narrative?

We access fiction in different ways. In the past, many people who couldn't read picked up stories, or narratives, from stained-glass windows in churches.

Long before that, our distant ancestors told stories about animals in cave paintings. Today millions, who might not want to read a book, follow TV serials closely.

 ## Stories

There are many different ways of telling stories. First you have to decide whose voice you are going to use to tell the story.

You can pretend to be a character in the story you're writing or telling – known as a first-person narrative.

 Openings of three first-person narratives

"Whether I shall turn out to be the hero of my own life, or whether that station shall be held by anybody else, these pages must show. To begin my life with the beginning of my life, I record that I was born (as I have been informed and believe) on a Friday at twelve o'clock at night. It was remarked that the clock began to strike and I began to cry simultaneously."

David Copperfield by Charles Dickens (1849/50)

"If our Anthony was telling this story, he'd start with the money. It always comes down to money, he says, so you might as well start there. He'd probably put, 'Once upon a time there were 229,370 little pounds sterling', and go on until he got to, 'and they all lived happily ever after in a high-interest bank account'. But he's not telling this story. I am."

Millions by Frank Cottrell Boyce (2004)

"I sat on the seat outside Sainsbury's with Digger, our dog, on his lead. We were waiting for Mum to finish the shopping because she'd promised to drop us off at my friend's house afterwards. Suddenly I noticed the green car."

'Mystery' by Joshua, aged 10 (2011)

Or you can tell your story as if you are an invisible person describing what the characters do and say, by looking in from right outside the story. This is called a third-person narrative.

Openings of three third-person narratives

"This is the story of the great war that Rikki-tikki-tavi fought single-handed through the bathrooms of the big bungalow in Segowlee cantonment. Darzee, the tailor-bird helped him, and Chuchundra the musk-rat, who never comes into the middle of the floor, but always creeps round by the wall, gave him advice; but Rikki-tikki did the real fighting."

'Rikki-tikki-tavi' from The Jungle Book by Rudyard Kipling (1894)

"Even the dead tell stories.

Sig looked across the cabin to where his father lay, waiting for him to speak, but his father said nothing, because he was dead."

Revolver by Marcus Sedgwick (2009)

"Lauren grabbed her kid sister's hand. She hated having to look after Ella, who was a real pain, but she had to stop her running into the road."

Unnamed story by Tiba, aged 11 (2011)

It is worth talking to young writers about first- and third-person narratives. What are the pros and cons of each? Although pupils may be used to reading or hearing stories told both ways, they may never have considered the differences.

For example:

 A first-person narrator can describe only what he or she has seen, heard or experienced. However there are ways around this: some professional writers add complicated devices such as letters, or the narrator being told about something which happened 'off stage' by another character.

A third-person narrator can tell the reader the thoughts and actions of any character, anywhere, and can – as the omniscient author – move in and out of as many situations as he or she wishes, like a fly on the wall.

Names for characters

Choosing names for characters in a story may not seem an important issue. But it is. Stories with plausible names are more credible.

How do writers choose names for their characters? It's important to talk to young writers about this. Credibility brings veracity.

 An elderly man who has worked all his life as a cleaner is unlikely to be called Romeo or Brooklyn, for example (as are two of David Beckham's sons). An old-fashioned name such as Jim or Bill is likely to be much more realistic.

Make the children aware that, as with many things, there are fashions in names, so that a particular name may become very popular for a while. Old names come back too. George, for example, is popular again for boys. So is Ruby for girls.

Names are an important part of story-telling. By way of practice, get the children to invent characters and then give them an appropriate name. Or give each pupil a

 Three quarters of a million girls were named Susan (and I should know) within the five years surrounding my birth date. My friends were called Linda, Anne, Mary, Roger and Ian.

But none of my contemporaries was named Alice, Olivia, Jack or Henry – as many children and teenagers are now.

name to work with – such as Doris, Panjit, Sasha, Ben, Cyril, Ophelia or Martin, and get him or her to invent a plausible character to fit the name.

 # Beginnings, middles and endings

A traditional fairy story begins '*Once upon a time ...*' and it ends '*And they all lived happily ever after.*' Anything which happens between these is the middle of the story.

Encourage the children to think of all stories as having a beginning and an ending, which together frame the story (although with the exception of the youngest children it will probably be more complex than a fairy story.)

 ## Starting stories

There are many ways of starting a story. For example, a writer can:

✓ introduce a character

 'Max was sitting on the sea wall, idly drumming his heels ...'

✓ set the scene

 'The bell rang and the schoolchildren burst noisily though the damp, grey-walled area into the panelled hall, where mid-morning snacks awaited them ...'

✓ describe a situation in which everything is not quite what it seems. This can tantalise the reader (then, in the next paragraph, the writer explains what is really happening)

 'They were being attacked on all sides. The noise rattled over their heads. This was life and death ... Nicky and Sanjay had always loved football. It was why they were friends ...'

✓ jump straight into unexplained dialogue, only later explaining who is speaking and why

' *"Let's go inside and find out."*

"Do you really think we should?"

"Yes, come on."

Ellie and Mia were standing outside Horniman's Museum in London. Ellie was insisting that one of the exhibits was a famous stuffed walrus. Mia didn't believe her.'

✓ make a mysterious statement, to make the reader continue reading

 'It was all the Queen's fault ...' or

'I have always adored peanut butter ...'

Ending stories

Stories can end in different ways too. For instance a writer might:

✓ spring a surprise (i.e. end the story with something the reader was not expecting)

For example, if two characters have been exploring a cave, the reader is probably waiting for them to discover something interesting and come out safely at the end of the story. Instead the writer could drown them as the tide comes in. If it's a love story it could end with the two people separating without the obvious 'happy ever after' ending.

✓ take the characters back to where they started

So, for example, Max is sitting on the sea wall at the end of the story, just as he was at the beginning.

✓ end with a joke

Some memorable story openings

"I have been in love with Titus Oates for quite a while now – which is ridiculous since he's been dead for ninety years."

Geraldine McCaughrean, The White Darkness (2005)

"Last night I dreamt I went to Manderley again."

Daphne Du Maurier, Rebecca (1938)

"All happy families are alike, but an unhappy family is unhappy after its own fashion."

Leo Tolstoy, Anna Karenina (1878)

"Things started to fall apart at home when my brother Jaja did not go to communion and Papa flung his heavy missal across the room and broke the figurines on the étagère."

Chimamanda Ngozi Adichie, Purple Hibiscus (2004)

"It is a truth universally acknowledged, that a single man in possession of a good fortune must be in want of a wife."

Jane Austen, Pride and Prejudice (1813)

"In the beginning God created the heaven and the earth."

'Genesis' from the Authorised Version of The Bible (translated 1611)

'The moral of this story is that parents are better news than you might think.' or

'And so, you see, it isn't usually a good idea to pit yourself against a challenge – whatever teachers, pushy parents and youth leaders might tell you.'

 # Dialogue

Nearly all stories have characters. And characters speak to each other.

So fiction writers create dialogue or conversation. Encourage young writers:

✓ to make it clear at all times who is speaking

✓ to capture the way a character would speak through the words given to them. For example, are the words spoken formal, colloquial, hesitant, confident, angry or calm?

✓ (as soon as they are able) to punctuate the characters' dialogue to ensure clarity. Start this process with a new line for each

 ## Avoiding 'said'

Avoid overuse of the ubiquitous *said* in dialogue. Here are some alternatives:

whispered	asked	proposed
bellowed	breathed	shouted
demanded	enquired	mumbled
questioned	exclaimed	grumbled
murmured	declaimed	growled
muttered	suggested	groaned

new speaker, even if the finer points of using speech marks lie a long way into the future.

 ## Plays

Children will often 'write' stories in the sense of inventing them, or making them up, without actually recording them in words on paper or on a computer.

Watch a group of under-7s playing any kind of 'make-believe'. They are actually writing (or doing what theatre people call 'devising') and directing short plays.

Try scribing the plays thus 'produced' by groups of young children, so that you have captured, or saved, the work. If you have a video camera, you could get the children to record each play.

Talk to the children about how playwrights work and show them how plays are usually set out on paper.

> A written play is really only a refined form of dialogue. Dialogue is an important part of nearly all fiction.

An example of written play text follows on the next page.

Conventions of written play texts

The following conventions apply to written play texts.

✓ Stage directions are given in italics.

✓ The names of characters are given in block capitals (i.e. upper case).

✓ The exact words to be spoken are written down ('direct speech'), without '*she said*', etc.

✓   A colon (:) is used to separate the characters' names from their words.

✓   Leave a line every time a different character speaks.

 These conventions may seem a bit fussy, but it's a good idea to draw children's attention to them and to talk about why they matter.

(The reason is that playwrights usually have to hand their work over to actors and directors, so the writer's intentions have to be as clear as possible.)

Here is an example of written play text.

They gather round a bowl.

PHYLLIS: If you have and were still young enough to be interested in everything ...

PETER: ... you'll find it almost impossible to resist ...

PHYLLIS: ... poking your finger in it, making a big dent.

She does so.

BOBBIE: Well if you have, you'll notice that slowly ...

PETER: ... but quite surely ...

PHYLLIS: ... the dent will disappear.

BOBBIE: And there, the dough will look exactly the same as it did before.

From E Nesbit's *The Railway Children*, adapted for the stage by Mike Kenny (Nick Hern Books, 2010).

The theatre presents great opportunities for creative writing.

You might show the children some plays by other playwrights, such as William Shakespeare, or the very simple *Dark Man* plays by Peter Lancett. The children don't need to read the plays (unless they particularly want to). But they should at least have heard of Shakespeare – and it's a good opportunity to see how plays are set out on the page.

 If a child (or a group of children) writes a play in school, ideally it should then be performed by another group of children, to see how well it 'works'. Changes to make it work better can than be negotiated.

A playwright makes plays just as a wheelwright makes (or traditionally made) wheels and a shipwright built ships.

That is why 'playwright' is spelled w-r-i-g-h-t and not w-r-i-t-e. Talk about this spelling quirk with the children. Once they have understood the reasons for it they will be less likely to make a mistake.

'Primary Voices' project

'Primary Voices' is a good example of how working with the play format can stimulate and enhance children's writing skills. It is an annual project run by Quicksilver Theatre in London, based at the New Diorama Theatre.

The project begins with playwriting workshops in primary schools for Year Six children (aged 10 – 11), with a theatre director and actors in the classroom. It culminates in a professional showcase, in a local theatre, of plays written by children.

> 'You cannot imagine the enjoyment and excitement of these Year Six pupils. Usually it is so difficult to motivate and keep a theme running with these teenagers who think they have outgrown the primary school but these pupils had grins as big as four year olds at Christmas time. In the SATs at Year Six in 2006 our writing results were better than our reading results.
>
> I have no hesitation in commending Primary Voices as a way of supporting the school to achieve expected standards of attainment.'
>
> *Head Teacher of a London primary school*

At the time of writing the project has been running in London for four years. There is an education pack free to download on the Quicksilver website (*www.quicksilvertheatre.co.uk/Productions-Primary-Voices.aspx*).

 ## Poetry

oems – usually known as narrative poems – tell
stories too.

The chief defect of Henry King
Was chewing little bits of string.
At last he swallowed some which tied
Itself in ugly knots inside.

Physicians of the utmost fame
Were called at once; but when they came
They answered, as they took their fees,
'There is no cure for this disease.

Henry will very soon be dead.'
His parents stood about his bed
Lamenting his untimely death,
When Henry, with his latest breath,

Cried, 'Oh, my Friends, be warned by me,
That breakfast, dinner, lunch, and tea
Are all the human frame requires ...'
With that, the wretched child expires.

'Henry King' by Hilaire Belloc, 1907

The wind was a torrent of darkness among the gusty trees,
The moon was a ghostly galleon tossed upon cloudy seas,
The road was a ribbon of moonlight over the purple moor,
And the highwayman came riding –
Riding – riding –
The highwayman came riding, up to the old inn-door.

From 'The Highwayman' by Alfred Noyes, 1913

> Way back in eighteen-fifty, when Americans were thrifty,
> The times were hard, so most folks had to toil;
> My mama, my pa and me labored hard to guarantee
> That we'd earn a living from the barren soil.
>
> *From 'Wagons West' by Roy Gerrard, 2000*

Children often like writing poetry, perhaps because it is:

✓ shorter than most prose

✓ freer. You can use words as imaginatively as you like

✓ easy to make it look attractive on the page

✓ a good medium for expressing feelings, and

✓ very personal.

Poet Sandy Brownjohn, who spends a lot of time working in schools, called one of her how-to books for teachers *Does it Have to Rhyme?* (Hodder and Stoughton, 1980) because it's the question she is most often asked by children.

The answer, of course, is '*no*'.

Although some poems tell stories, many poems do not. Other forms of poetry include:

• friendship poems
• lyric poetry
• poems about animals
• funny poetry – which can be used to great effect with children, and
• descriptions of, and thoughts about, things which move or interest the poet.

Some poetry is very structured. For example:

- the **sonnet**, which has 14 lines and a specific rhyme pattern
- the **haiku**, which has just 17 syllables
- **traditional ballads**, which are written in four-line verses. Many poets (such as Coleridge in *The Ancient Mariner*) have imitated it.

Other poetry is very free, using fluid, irregular rhythmic patterns and little or no rhyme.

A lot of poetry is written in blank verse – from Milton's *Paradise Lost* to most of the work of the late Ted Hughes.

In this context the word 'blank' simply means unrhymed.

What NOT to do

And finally, an object lesson in what NOT to do.

Brian Jacques, author of the popular *Redwall* series of children's novels, died in February 2011, aged 71.

According to his obituary in The Daily Telegraph (8th February 2011), Jacques, an enthusiastic reader, 'soon demonstrated a precocious writing talent of his own. Aged 10, he was told to write a story about animals and turned in a tale about a bird that cleaned a crocodile's teeth. His teacher refused to believe that a boy so young could write so imaginatively and caned Brian when he insisted he had not copied it.'

Fortunately for all the children who later enjoyed his books, this did not put Jacques off writing for life.

Caning, of course, has long gone, thank goodness. But the anecdote is a useful reminder of the importance of being positive about children's efforts.

If there's doubt – always give the child the benefit of it.

3 Fiction, Plays and Poems

Practical Teaching Ideas

 ## Interesting objects

 Show the children an interesting object (which you have probably brought from home or borrowed) and talk to them about it. Encourage them to make up stories based on the object.

> For example, if you show the children an old pocket watch, they might imagine the person who first owned it, and weave a story about who that person was and their relationship with the watch.
>
> Or if you show them a blue and white willow pattern plate, the children might imagine a story being told by the figures and drawings on the plate.
>
> A football shirt could be a starting point for a story about the owner of the shirt (a player or a fan) or about the club.

Other possible objects to stimulate a story include:

- a beach pebble or shell
- an unusual shoe or boot
- an old fork, spoon or knife, bearing engraved initials
- a coloured or patterned scarf
- any sort of hat
- a thimble
- an old tool, such as screwdriver that has clearly been in use for many years
- an old mobile phone, or
- an elegant cup and saucer.

Pictures

I'm a great believer in collecting pictures from old magazines. Weekend newspaper supplements are ideal.

 The pictures won't last for more than a lesson or two, but there are plenty more where they came from. Look for striking, interesting, quirky, funny or ambiguous photographs. Advertisements are a rich source.

 Give the pictures out to a class – either one picture for each child or to the children working in pairs. Alternatively you could use one picture for whole-class discussion.

 Ask the children to fictionalise the picture – either as individuals, in pairs or in conversation with you.

 Of course this is an activity that parents, carers and guardians can do just as easily at home.

Pictures offer many opportunities to start a narrative.

 Ask questions based on the content of the pictures – such as *'Why has he just come though that door?' 'What's she looking at?' 'How long has that child been waiting?' 'Who are those people and what are their names?' 'Why is that woman laughing / scowling/ crying/ shouting (or whatever)?'*

 Gradually build a narrative which can be written – as a story, a play or a poem.

Alternatively you could present the children with a story starter, based on the picture.
For example:
'The figure sprinted away from the angry crowd and headed towards a gap between the buildings.'

Postcards

✏ Don't throw away those coloured picture postcards that people send when on holiday. Encourage the children to save them too – and bring them to school. Ask your friends and relations to pass postcards they receive on to you as well, so that you can use them in school (as long as there isn't anything too rude or personal written on the back, of course!).

✏ Postcards often show views such as the sea, mountains, lakes, hills, rivers and so on. Or they depict famous, interesting and/or beautiful buildings. Some celebrate local life, customs and traditions, such as Swiss cows with bells round their necks, kilted Scottish highlanders playing bagpipes or cheese making in Derbyshire. Items in museums and art galleries often feature on postcards too. So do people in distinctive roles such as the Yeomen Warders at The Tower of London, or young women in floral garlands in Hawaii. Many postcards feature plants and animals, too.

A collection of postcards is a rich seam of fictional inspiration. And they're easy to store and handle.

✏ Give the postcards out. Encourage the children to discuss the pictures, to imagine what might be happening and then to write up their narrative.

Here's an idea:

As you shake your morning breakfast cereal from the box, out tumbles a small, red envelope with the words 'Open me now!' stamped on it. Inside, there is a list of instructions that you must carry out 'before night falls'.

Write the story of your day.

Fan fiction

✐ If a young reader is smitten with a book he or she has read or has heard read aloud, then one way of encouraging writing is to suggest writing 'spin-off' stories. In other words, for the child to make up new, original stories about the author's original characters, or based on places or incidents found in the book. Because this works on the reader's feelings (as a fan of the book or series of books), it is known as 'fan fiction'.

 Hundreds of thousands of readers have, for instance, written their own Harry Potter stories.

✐ You could also ask the children to do the same thing based around their favourite TV soaps or computer games. Their stories could focus on a favourite character.

Tie-ins with writing events

 ## National Storytelling Week

✐ National Storytelling Week (*www.sfs.org.uk/nsw*) is a UK event, run annually in late January/early February by the Society for Storytelling. In 2010 the event involved 16,500 people. Hundreds of schools take part each year, and events are also run by museums, art galleries, zoos and other community institutions, including local heritage centres and radio stations – even shopping centres.

✐ National Storytelling Week can be a good launchpad for creative writing in school. If you want to run a National Storytelling Week event in your school – and inspire your pupils to create more stories of their own – the Society will:

• help you to find a storyteller near you

- advise you about promoting your event
- provide official logos and other resources, and
- report your event in its magazine, *Storylines*.

 ## National Novel Writing Month

✐ For older students, National Novel Writing Month (*http://www.nanowrimo.org/*), held for the thirty days of November each year, offers some engaging writing challenges.

✐ The aim is to write a 50,000 word (approximately 175 page) novel by 11:59:59 on November 30, starting from scratch on 1st November.

✐ It's intended to be a fun event, with the emphasis firmly on quantity rather than quality.

> From the Nanowrimo website:
>
> '*Valuing enthusiasm and perseverance over painstaking craft, NaNoWriMo is a novel-writing program for everyone who has thought fleetingly about writing a novel but has been scared away by the time and effort involved.*'

✐ The website for this international event contains plenty of support and advice for those prepared to give it a try.

 # Limericks

Children often enjoy writing limericks because they are short, creative and have the potential to be funny – or even rude.

✏ But first you will need to read and discuss a few limericks with them because they will not – obviously – be able to write in a genre which is unfamiliar to them.

✏ This one, like most limericks, tells a mini-story:

> There was a young lady from Tottenham
> Who'd no manners, or else she'd forgotten 'em.
> At tea at the vicar's,
> She tore off her knickers,
> Because she said she felt 'ot in 'em.

There are more children's limericks to read and share at *www.kidsonthenet.org.uk/create/limericks.cfm*.

This is advice from Bruce Lansky at *www.gigglepoetry.com*:

Ideas for new limericks can come from almost anywhere. For example, your city, state, country, or name. If your name is Tim or Jim, you could write something like this:

A Clumsy Young Fellow Named Tim
1.   *There once was a fellow named Tim* (A)
2.   *Whose dad never taught him to swim.* (A)
3.   *He fell off a dock* (B)
4.   *And sunk like a rock.* (B)
5.   *And that was the end of him.* (A)

Notice the rhyme pattern (AABBA) and the rhythm pattern (3 'dums', 3 'dums', 2 'dums', 2 'dums', 3 'dums').

Five simple steps to writing a limerick

1 Pick a boy's or girl's name that has one syllable (like Bill, Tim, Dick, Sue or Jill):

There once was a fellow (or young girl) named _____ (say, Jill).

2 Now make a list of words that rhyme with the name you chose. For *Jill*, your list of rhyming words might include: *hill, drill, pill, skill, bill, will* and *ill.*

3 Now write the second line using one of the rhyming words. Here's an example:

Who freaked at the sight of a drill.

(Notice that the last words in the first two lines rhyme, and both the first and second lines contain 3 'dums', or beats.)

4 Now think of an interesting story. What could happen to someone scared of a drill? What if Jill had to go to the dentist? Here's what might happen in the third and fourth lines.

She brushed every day
So her dentist would say,

(Notice that *day* and *say*, the last words in the third and fourth lines, both rhyme. And notice there are 2 'dums', or beats, in each line.)

5 Now go back to the list of words rhyming with *Jill* to find one that can end the poem. Here's an example:

Your teeth are quite perfect – no bill!

Here's the poem we just wrote:

There once was a young girl named Jill
Who freaked at the sight of a drill.
She brushed every day
So her dentist would say,
Your teeth are so perfect – no bill!

Now try it yourself!

Colour

> The Colours
>
> What is pink? A rose is pink
> By the fountain's brink.
> What is red? A poppy's red
> In its barley bed.
> What is blue? The sky is blue
> Where the clouds float thro'.
> What is white? A swan is white,
> Sailing in the light.
> What is yellow? Pears are yellow,
> Rich and ripe and mellow.
> What is green? The grass is green,
> With small flowers between.
> What is violet? Clouds are violet
> In the summer twilight.
> What is orange? Why, an orange –
> Just an orange.
>
> *Christina Rossetti (1830-1894)*

✎ This poem focuses on colours in nature. Share it with the children and talk to them about colours in the man-made world too. You might, for example, mention:

- colours of cars
- post boxes
- supermarket logos and theme colours, or
- fluorescent safety wear.

✎ Encourage the children to create a colour poem of their own. It could, at first, be as simple as a glorified list linking the colours and the items:

- red post van ...
- lime workmen ...
- white Fiat ...

Expanding to:
- Vermilion post van ...
- Shiny lime workmen ...
- Snowy white Fiat ...

And on to:
- The shiny lime-clad workmen dig and trudge
- As the vermilion post van slides by
- And the snowy white Fiat shoots past ...

 Another possibility is to get the children to use Christina Rossetti's framework, but to choose their own colours and items:
- What is lime? A roadman's coat is lime
- Digging through tarmac in time.
- What is red? A post box is red
- Like a cut just bled ...

You – and the children – could of course create colour poetry rooted in nature, as Rossetti did. You might do this as a class activity to create a single poem, with different children making contributions and everyone chipping in to refine the work.

Other sources of colour in nature could include:
- butterflies
- vegetables (such as carrots, aubergines, butternut squashes, peas, or red, green and yellow peppers)
- fruits (such as grapes, kiwis, bananas, strawberries and blackcurrants)
- tree bark
- tropical fish
- gems, such as amethyst, emerald and ruby, and
- birds.

Pictures could be useful here, too.

Haikus

'Haiku' is a traditional form of Japanese poetry. Haiku poems consist of 3 lines. The first and last lines of a haiku have 5 syllables and the middle line has 7 syllables. The lines rarely rhyme.

Here's a self-defining haiku:

> *I am first with five*
> *Then seven in the middle –*
> *Five again to end.*

Children tend to like haikus because they are both short and easy.

Try getting the children to write haikus as riddles. In other words, they write the haiku and then ask the rest of the class 'What am I?' For example:

> *Green and speckled legs*
> *Hop on logs and lily pads*
> *Splash in cool water.*

Or

> *In a pouch I grow,*
> *On a southern continent –*
> *Strange creatures I know.*

You can also ask the children to write haikus about things which interest them, such as this one about snow:

> Snowflakes are our friends
> They descend when winter comes
> Making white blankets.
>
> *by Kaitlyn Guenther*

Or this about beaches:

> Sand scatters the beach
> Waves crash on the sandy shore
> Blue water shimmers.
>
> *by Kaitlyn Guenther*

Plays from known stories – Key Stage 1 (ages 5 – 7)

One way of getting children to embark on writing play texts is to start with a familiar story. With younger pupils this could be (for example) a fairy story, such as *Little Red Riding Hood* or *The Three Bears*, or a book story such as *Bedtime Without Arthur* (Jessica Meserve, Anderson Press, 2009) or *The Tiger Who Came to Tea* (Judith Kerr, first published 1968, new edition HarperCollins 2006).

Start by getting the children to 'play' the story they know. Repeat it several times. Then they can begin to write their dramatisation – possibly with an adult as scribe.

> At this stage you can begin to talk about how plays are written down, so that the children's instructions are clear for the actors to follow.

Introduce the idea of stage directions. When the wolf first spots Red Riding Hood in the wood, where is he? Is he behind a tree? Or crouching beside a bush? Standing on the path? And how is he behaving? Is he smiling? Frowning? Is he looking impatient, hungry or gleeful? The playwright(s) or play devisers have to make their wishes and plans clear.

Plays from known stories – Key Stages 2 and 3 (ages 7 – 14)

 To introduce students to the idea of adapting stories into plays, in a perfect world you would start by reading a book such as *The Railway Children* (E. Nesbit, 1906) or *Goodnight Mister Tom* (Michelle Magorian,1981) with the students and then you would show them (or take them to) some sort of dramatisation (a live play or film) of the book. You could then talk to them about the sorts of changes that need to be made in adapting a novel into a play. You could then invite the students to have a go at dramatising part of a novel for themselves.

In the real world, however, this might not be possible. Instead, talk the students through how playwrights have to visualise the story on stage, and then imagine how it could be retold.

Choose a section of a book that the students know well – or get them to choose a suitable passage – and try it out. Pay particular attention to:

✓ the conventions of setting out plays; and

✓ stage directions.

> At this stage you can begin to talk about how plays are written down, so that the students' instructions are clear for the actors to follow.

If the students collaborate on a text to produce a script, and if each group works on a different text, they can later take turns to perform each others' playlets.

Here are some suggestions for books, extracts from which might lend themselves to adaptation as mini-plays.

The Graveyard Book by Neil Garman (Bloomsbury, 2009)
Revolver by Marcus Sedgwick (Orion, 2009)
Ronnie's War by Bernard Ashley (Frances Lincoln Children's Books, 2010)
The Silver Sword by Ian Serraillier (1956, now Red Fox)
Tamar by Mal Peet (Walker, 2004)
Skellig by David Almond (Hodder, 1997)
The Ghost of Thomas Kempe by Penelope Lively (1972, now Egmont).

Plays from other sources

✎ Apart from books, there are many other sources of stories, or narratives, that can be used as material to adapt into plays.

✎ Comics are pretty dramatic and full of stories. Can you get the students to retell any of these as plays?

✎ Computer games are potentially another good source. (There is more on this in Chapter 5.)

✎ Ask the students if they can make plays from stories passed down to them in their families.

For example, a story about Grandad leaving his umbrella on a bus, and when he went to the lost property office to ask about it, Nan was in charge. That's how they met.

He asked her out and they went to a dance the next day – and married the year after.

✐ Older students might find sources for stories in newspapers or by reading the news on the Internet. *www.bbc.co.uk/news* is a good news website for this purpose.

Made-up plays

Don't forget to encourage children to create plays straight from their own imagination.

✐ Such a play (or playlet) might be:

✓ rooted in family life (e.g. a family in a car, setting off on holiday)

✓ fantasy (wizards, witches, space, dinosaurs – what you will)

✓ a school scene (e.g. bullying, support when something terrible happens to a classmate, or something much more dramatic)

✓ something historical

✓ geographical and current (e.g. involving a recent, well-publicised natural disaster).

 Most of the ideas suggested here for plays could work just as well as stories or poems. Invite and encourage the children to respond to ideas in whatever genre they choose.

When you are trying to unlock the writer in every child, it's essential to accept that the inner writer is an individualistic beast.

4 Writing Non-fiction

4 Writing Non-fiction

The Issues

Fiction 'versus' non-fiction

As we have seen, some children are simply not interested in reading or writing fiction. It's important to accept that we're all different and, as the proverb has it: *One person's meat is another's poison.*

I still maintain, however, along with many respected psychologists, that everyone needs fiction.

It's simply that those who don't want to read or write it get it from other sources – from watching TV soaps, repeating narrative jokes or playing computer games with narrative elements.

My father swore all his life that he hadn't read a fiction book since he left school. '*All lies and I can't see the point of it,*' he would say. Yet he loved to write and was good at it.

In adult life he had a number of sparky, witty, factual and comment pieces published in magazines and journals.

The lesson is clear. If we want to unlock the writer in every child, we have to lead each individual to as many forms of writing as we can and carefully respect every aspect of writing.

And that's not easy, actually. I'm a professional writer and journalist. I earn my living by writing words which other people pay to read. But I don't write fiction (although I read a great deal of it). If I tell someone at a party that I write books, eyes light up and the next eager question is 'What sort of books do you write?'

 They want, of course, to discover that they're talking to the author of the latest blockbuster they've seen on an airport bookstand. Their eyes glaze as soon as I tell them that I write mostly 'how-to' books for education professionals and parents, English textbooks and a lot of journalism.

It's as if non-fiction is a substandard genre which somehow doesn't quite count.

Signalling alternatives to fiction

Given that general attitude, it's a bit of a challenge to persuade a child that, even if most of their classmates are happy to have a go at fiction, there are other things to be written which are just as valid as a creative means of self expression – and, although the child may not be aware of it, a way of developing better use of language and improved literacy skills.

When you suggest writing tasks for pupils, make sure you always suggest a range of options so that the resistant-to-fiction writers have an avenue to explore.

If, for example, you have shown the children some shells and seaweed, and have invited them to write a story about the sea, or a story set at the seaside, you might also discuss the following with the children.

✓ Ask them to describe an occasion when they went somewhere by sea. The description could be in the form of a letter or email.

✓ Ask the children why they think people like to spend holidays near the sea. They should write their opinions down.

✓ Ask the children to write a review of any book they have read, or film they have seen, which involved the sea.

✓ Ask the children to write about any aspect of the sea in any way that they wish.

Always include a wide-open option: 'any aspect' or 'in any way you wish'.

The following is taken from the UK Key Stage 3 National Curriculum Programme of Study ('Range and content'). Apart from any authority it has as curriculum guidance, it serves as a very useful reminder for teachers working with children in their writing.

'In their writing pupils should:
a) develop ideas, themes, imagery, settings and/or characters when writing to imagine, explore and entertain
b) analyse and evaluate subject matter, supporting views and opinions with evidence
c) present ideas and views logically and persuasively
d) explain or describe information and ideas relevantly and clearly.
The forms for such writing should be drawn from different kinds of:
e) stories, poems, play scripts, autobiographies, screenplays, diaries, minutes, accounts, information leaflets, plans, summaries, brochures, advertisements, editorials, articles and letters conveying opinions, campaign literature, polemics, reviews, commentaries, articles, essays and reports.'

Expressing opinions in writing

If you ask children what they think about something, most will tell you in a reasonably forthcoming way.

For example:

*   How do you think school dinners could be improved?
*   What do you think about school uniform?
*   What are your views about homework?

Children like to be consulted. It's why school councils and discussion forums work so well. Children feel that their voices are being heard.

Well they can also be 'heard' in writing.

Older students might be concerned about local amenities, job and training opportunities, the relevance (or otherwise) of the school curriculum, school buildings – and a host of other issues.

Encourage them to express these in letters or emails to local or national newspapers. (Almost all publications now accept and prefer 'letters for publication' by email.)

Teach the students:

Are there local (or wider) issues that are bugging the pupils? Is it litter in the streets, or too few school crossing patrols at key points by schools? Or perhaps it's environmental matters.

✓ to express their point of view as simply and as directly as possible

✓ not to use vague expressions which add nothing – e.g. 'I am writing to ... ' at the beginning. That's obvious and doesn't need saying

✓ to keep sentences – and indeed the whole letter – short

✓ to cite evidence, if relevant

✓ to refer to whatever triggered the letter in the first instance – e.g. an item in the newspaper.

I f a child's letter is published in a newspaper or magazine, or on a website or in a book, then make something of it. Celebrate the success. It will do wonders for the writer's self esteem and sense of achievement.

Cut the letter out, or print it. Display it in the classroom and/or store it in some sort of portfolio or folder (physical or electronic) which collects and celebrates the child's achievements. Talk about it. Read it to the class. Read it in assembly. Put it on the school's intranet and website. Showcase it on the school's virtual learning environment (VLE) if there is one. Tell parents about it – via newsletters, e-letters or whatever you use to share the school's news with its community.

 ## Letters from children

> Too many children are taken to school by car. It makes them lazy and they get fat. And their parents' cars cause traffic jams.
>
> If you live quite near the school then you should walk. My little brother and I walk every day and it takes us about 15 minutes. My mum walks with us and says it's good for her, too. I like chatting to Mum as we walk.
>
> *Alfie Jones, aged 7*

 Always get young letter/email writers to put their age on their work. Most recipients are likely to respond positively – by publishing the letter for example – if they know that the writer is young. Many of them want to encourage young writers as much as education professionals and parents do.

Far more scientists believe in global warming than don't ('*Global Warming sceptics speak out*' 17 January 2011).

Anyone who disregards the evidence of climate change – the now penetrable North West Passage, adapting migration patterns in birds, unusual and extreme weather incidents all over the world – is simply copping out of acknowledging the truth.

I suppose if you're 50 or so you can afford to be complacent. But it's my generation which will really feel the impact.

So it's time to talk constructively about this and work out what, if anything, we can do to lessen the effect of climate change in the rest of the 21st century and beyond.

Charlotte Marciniak, aged 15

 In 2010 an article appeared in The Times which was negative about the town of Hastings, on the south coast of England, described by the journalist as a very run-down town.

A group of Hastings primary schoolchildren took exception to this and wrote to The Times newspaper, asking the journalist to visit them, so that they could show all the positive things in Hastings.

They got a result. Although the original journalist had been posted abroad, another Times journalist, Damian Whitworth, accepted the invitation and spent a day touring the town with the children, their class teacher and head teacher. He then wrote a second article about Hastings, which was published in January 2011, praising and quoting the children and being reasonably up-beat about what they had shown him.

It was a fine example of a good, practical outcome from children expressing their opinions in writing. The children may even, through their action, have helped to sway public opinions a little about their town.

 Closed and open questions

When you propose topics for discussion (and for writing), be aware of the difference between closed and open questions.

Newspapers offer opportunities for children to express their opinions.

 Share published letters with the pupils – and remember that many a good 'letter to the editor' is a response to a letter already published.

So another approach would be *'Just listen to this ...'* and then *'What do we feel about this?'* and finally *'Does anyone want to write an answer?'*

A closed question, such as *'Do you like school dinners?'* or *'Is school uniform a good idea?'* simply invites a shy or taciturn child to say 'yes' or 'no'.

Rather, start questions which might develop into subjects for writing – with words such as *'How'* and *'What'*, and expressions such as *'What do you think about ... ?'* and *'How could ... ?'* These kinds of questions – open questions – are far more likely to get an extended answer.

Remember that letters intended for publication are often written collaboratively, as in the case of the Hastings children. Two or three pupils might work together, pooling their views and hammering out together what they want to say.

This is particularly easy to do on a computer, because the writers can keep amending and refining their work. The finished letter should, of course, carry both, or all, names.

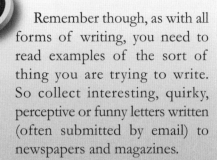

Remember though, as with all forms of writing, you need to read examples of the sort of thing you are trying to write. So collect interesting, quirky, perceptive or funny letters written (often submitted by email) to newspapers and magazines.

Other forms of opinion writing

Writing letters to newspapers on specific issues is a beneficial exercise, but it's useful also to move children on – for example, to magazine or newspaper-type articles and blogs. These are all examples of 'opinion' writing, where children can express and articulate their views on specific topics.

Collect, share and display a range of opinion articles and blogs. (Children won't be able to write such articles if they haven't read any to start with.) With hard copy you can do this in the traditional way using notice boards and folders, but laminate or protect them if they're going on the wall so they don't get too tatty too quickly. Plastic storage pockets are useful for keeping ring binders tidy.

To store blogs and online articles, create a designated favourites list with links – or each pupil could create their own.

Look for (and encourage pupils to look for) writing which comments on things which interest or concern them.

You can often persuade a pupil who has written, say, a hundred-word letter (Charlotte Marciniak's letter on page 111 has 109 words), to develop an argument on the same topic into, perhaps, a 300-word article.

Other forms of opinion writing pupils might be encouraged to try include:

 ## Essays

An essay – from the French word *essayer* (to try) – is a written work in which the writer *tries* to work out what they think about a particular topic. Many 'thinkpiece' articles in newspapers are, in fact, essays.

Blogs

(An abbreviation of *web-log*.) Consider setting up a class blog, through which different class members can express their views. Others – including you, parents and others – could then post comments on the blog posts.

Poems

> **M**any famous poems express views, even if they don't do so overtly.

Much (if not all) of the war poetry of Wilfred Owen, for example, criticises the sending of innocent young men to their deaths on battlefields of the First World War in 1914-18.

For another example, this poem expresses a view about caged animals in old-fashioned zoos:

> The Tigress
>
> They trapped her in the Indian hills
> And put her in a box; and though so young
> The dockers quailed to hear her voice
> As she made war on every bolt and thong.
> Now she paces, sleeps on her ledge,
> Glares, growls, excretes, gnaws lumps of meat,
> Sun and shadow in the iron bars
> Dropping about her and a listless mate.
>
> *Clifford Dyment (1914-1971)*

Songs

Many modern 'folk' songs express clear views about perceived injustices (these are so-called 'protest songs').

Protest songs really came into their own in the 1960s with songs such as Bob Dylan's *Blowin' in the Wind* and the much older *We Shall Overcome*, which Joan Baez popularised. Hymns, or traditional spirituals, such as *The Ink is Black* are a close relation and are likely to be known to some students.

> It is easier to write a protest song if you make the words fit a fairly simple tune you already know – such as a nursery rhyme, hymn, tune from a musical, a TV theme tune or whatever. Then you simply write at the top: 'To the tune of ...'.

 # Writing reviews

Young people can often enjoy reading fiction without wanting to write fiction themselves. But that does not prevent them writing a review of a fiction book that they have read. Such a review expresses an opinion – even though it is about a work of fiction.

There is a knack to writing worthwhile fiction reviews and, as with all writing work, it comes only through reading plenty of examples of other people's reviews.

So the usual advice prevails: **collect**, **share**, **discuss** and **display**.

> The key thing is to persuade young reviewers to go beyond '*I thought this book was brilliant because I liked the characters and would recommend it to anyone my age*' and to say something specific about the book – without, of course, revealing all its secrets.

Book reviews: DOs and DON'Ts

Do

- ✓ Put the book's full title, author and publisher (with year of publication) at the top.

- ✓ Say something about the book's setting – e.g. London during World War Two, a farm in present-day Cornwall or a fantasy world in which two alien tribes are in conflict.

- ✓ Mention some of the characters and say whether they are interesting, well-described, boring, etc.

- ✓ Refer to at least one incident in the book.

- ✓ Mention the author by name and comment on what he or she has achieved in the book.

- ✓ Make it clear whether or not you enjoyed the book – and why.

Don't

- ✗ Try to retell the whole story.

- ✗ Give away too much of the story. Certainly don't give away the ending.

- ✗ Make your review too long. Three hundred words is usually plenty.

Why not put a copy of this on the class noticeboard?

You can also, of course, invite pupils to write review of films, television programmes, computer games, live shows (such as plays or musicals), or even restaurants and cafes.

Another idea is to ask the students to write the script of a trailer for a book they have read, and then act it out, recording the result on video.

 This adds interest because the result is more than just a piece of writing. Students also need to get to grips with the differences between something that is written to be read and something that is written to be heard.

Writing for practical purposes

In schools, writing is not the exclusive province of the English, or literacy, lessons. 'Writing' must not be limited in this way.

Different curriculum areas require students to write in different styles and for different purposes. They might be asked, for example, to:

- make factual notes (about, say, a historical incident or, for a geography lesson, a country's crops)
- record the method, observations and conclusions in an experiment in (for example) science or sports studies, or
- write instructions (for example, a recipe for something devised or designed in food technology or cookery).

These are arguably less creative writing forms than some of the writing we've been discussing, because they tend to require a very specific format over which the writer has no choice. There are conventions – such as listing ingredients at the top of a recipe – which have to be learned. Nevertheless, these forms are part of the writing which every student is required to know and they should be valued.

Most important, students need to become adept at writing for these various kinds of practical purposes.

If a student is writing the recipe for a dish he or she has created, encourage him or her to write a couple of creative sentences at the top, just as many professional recipe book writers do. This could be about how the dish tastes, where the writer got the idea from or what to serve it with – or almost anything else. (The books written by Nigella Lawson are particularly useful in this regard.)

 As always, it's a good idea to make sure that recipe writers have read some examples by others – and that means cookery books or food-related articles from newspapers, magazines or the Internet.

4 Writing Non-fiction

Practical Teaching Ideas

Earliest memories

When it comes to creative writing, memory and imagination are a writer's two greatest assets.

- Talk to the children – of any age – about what they can remember from the past, especially the time when they were very small.

- Don't forget that memories can be happy or sad, of course.

 A child I know well (now aged nine) can just remember her great-granny, who died when she was two. She has told me several times, 'I can remember Granny Mollie lying in bed in the hospital with white sheets and she lifted up her head and said "Hello Jasmine."'

A child might remember, for example:

- his or her first day at school
- getting lost on one occasion
- his or her first best friend
- getting into trouble
- moving house
- a nursery, playgroup or childminder
- a particularly memorable holiday
- a memorable birthday party
- a particular Christmas, or presents he or she received
- the birth of a brother or sister
- being frightened by something
- visiting relations
- favourite toys, or
- an accident (happening to, or to somebody close to, him or her).

Ask the children to choose one of these recollections and write a short piece about some of what they remember.

This is, of course, the beginning of 'life' writing, or autobiography, and a child who enjoys it can be encouraged to develop it into something longer.

Obituaries

Explain to the children that an obituary is a brief biography of someone which appears in a newspaper or magazine, or on a website, after that person has died. Find some obituaries for the pupils to read.

Then try offering this task:

Imagine that during the course of your long life you have become famous for something. Use your imagination to think of a brief outline of your rise to fame. Then pretend that you are the journalist who has been told to write your obituary.

Now write your own obituary. This should be a brief account of your achievements, beginning with when and where you were born.

 Point out to the students that their obituary needs to be balanced. It's fine to talk about the person's strengths and achievements, but there might be bad things to record as well.

A room all for you

Here's a useful activity that goes beyond just writing. It's a way of getting students to imagine how they could use a space if money were no object.

 Ask the students to imagine that they have just moved into a much larger house or flat. They have been given a bedroom but there is also a spare room, which they have been told they can use in any way they like. In addition, they have won a large sum of money in a competition, so they can spend what they like on it.

 Ask them to draw a plan of the room, showing the doors, windows, radiators, etc. They should show the dimensions of the room.

 Working in pairs, ask the students to discuss how to make best use of the room (which they don't have to sleep in, remember). What would they use the room for? What is needed to achieve this? They should then draw the furnishings and equipment onto their plan.

 Then ask the students to write a letter (or an email) to a friend, describing the room and how they are going to use it.

School science experiments offer opportunities for different styles of writing.

 # Science experiment in two versions

✐ Most older students find themselves undertaking science experiments at school. An example of such an experiment would be the addition of iodine to a cut potato which, if it turned black, would indicate the presence of starch; this being compared with other potatoes that are dabbed with different substances which do not turn them black.

✐ Experiments of this type usually need to be written up formally afterwards. This involves 'objective', factual writing describing what was done, without emotive adjectives and without the used of the first person or the active voice. So '*Three potatoes were cut in half*' rather than '*We cut three potatoes in half*'.

✐ Then get the students to write in the opposite style. So instead of an objective, factual account, get them to write an imaginative description of the same activity, making it as entertaining, as exciting and as unscientific as possible. Such as – '*Well, there we were in the science lab chopping up spuds, but instead of turning them into tasty chips, our teacher wanted us to ...*'

A s well as being fun, this activity helps to highlight the differences between objective, scientific writing and subjective writing.

Fun with factual notes

✐ There are always occasions at school when students are required to record facts. We're a long way from Mr Gradgrind's '*Facts, facts and nothing but the facts*' in Charles Dickens's *Hard Times*, but nonetheless facts are part of education and students are quite often asked to write them down – usually by hand on paper, but sometimes typing them on a computer.

✐ A student who has just learned (for example) the location, length and economic importance of the Mississippi River might be asked to write half a page of succinct facts about the river. This information might be distilled from a teaching session, a presentation on a whiteboard or a research exercise involving the library and/or the Internet.

 Try asking the students to write about the Mississippi in any way they wish.

It could be a poem about old steamers, a comment on the romance of a river so much longer than anything we have in the UK, the river itself telling its own story from rising in the north to reaching its delta in the 'deep south' – or anything else the student wants to write, once all restrictions are lifted.

When making notes it's essential for the students to distil the material and record the essence, creating no more than a brief summary.

> ✏ But once that's done there's also scope for a different sort of creative writing.

 ## Book reviews published online

The Carnegie Medal has been awarded annually for a children's book since 1936. Past winners include *Pigeon Post* by Arthur Ransome, *The Borrowers* by Mary Norton, *The Owl Service* by Alan Garner and *The Graveyard Book* by Neil Gaiman. The award scheme is now run by CILIP (Chartered Institute of Librarians and Information Professionals).

The judges are a large panel of children's librarians who announce their shortlist of 5 – 8 books each April, choosing from books published between January and August the previous year.

> ✏ In recent years many schools have signed up to be Carnegie Medal shadowers. That means that, once the shortlist has been announced, the students read the books, discuss them in their schools and post reviews on CILIP's shadowing website. CILIP provides advice and support materials for those wanting to take part.

Crucially these students get to see their work published, so there's a real sense of achievement.

> ✏ When the winner is announced in June, pupils who have shadowed the prize take a real interest, because they have been involved and have likely already chosen their own winner.

In a way this is the literary equivalent of watching the fortunes of the football team you support.

The only resources needed are copies of the shortlisted books. The shadowing site is at *www.carnegiegreenaway.org.uk/shadowingsite*.

Film, TV and theatre reviews

People read reviews of plays, films and other performances for two main reasons:

✓ They are not likely to see the film or play themselves, but want to know more about it.

✓ They are considering going to see the work and want to know how good it is before they decide.

W riting reviews is an excellent exercise in writing for a purpose. The purpose is clear and the writing needs to be focused. Any views need to be fully supported. But in addition there is scope for creative interpretation and the expression of opinions.

Children and older students need to read some reviews before they can write them – but don't show them a review of the play or film you want them to review, because it will colour their views.

Share reviews of some relevant plays, films and other performances with the students. These could be reviews of current hit films, or a local theatre show, for example.

There are many reviews of plays and films on the Internet, too. Some sites such as *www.londontheatre.co.uk* and *www.totalfilm.com/ reviews* are entirely devoted to reviews. Most newspapers also publish their reviews online – often before they appear in the printed newspaper.

I often write professional reviews of plays for 'The Stage' newspaper (*www.thestage.co.uk/reviews*), which means attending press nights alongside leading critics from national newspapers. I write my review as soon as I get home, or first thing the next morning, and it has to be based entirely on my own response.

Even if someone has written an 'overnight', so that there is a review of the previous evening's play in the newspaper on my breakfast table, I do not allow myself to look at it until I have written my own and hit the 'send' button.

Young critics need to impose the same discipline on themselves, or they will not be able to write impartially.

Remember that any of the following could be reviewed:
- plays in venues outside school
- concerts of all types
- theatre-in-education productions which come into school
- films seen in or out of school
- DVDs
- TV programmes of all sorts
- circus performances
- street theatre
- puppet theatre
- computer games, and
- pantomimes.

Role-modelling can really help to unlock writers, particularly if you're male and you have reluctant boys in the group. Show them that writing's a cool thing for men to do too.

If you ask students to write reviews of something the whole class has shared – such as a film – then make sure *you* write a review too, and share it with the students.

Reading other children's reviews

Reading reviews written by other children is a great leveller, since these are not written by professional reviewers and therefore they aren't perceived by other children to have any particular authority. (Children will be less likely to disagree with a review published in a Sunday newspaper, for example.)

A good source of theatre reviews written by other children is The Unicorn Theatre in London. It is currently London's only purpose-built theatre for children and young people. It opened in 2005.

The theatre has a Young Critics' Programme, which is open to state secondary schools in the UK. The programme aims to encourage young people to think critically about a production they have seen at the theatre. The young critics are invited to press night alongside professional journalists, and later they submit their reviews to Unicorn. Some of the reviews are published on Unicorn's website (*www.unicorntheatre.com /for_schools /young_critics_programme*). These reviews are a useful resource for developing critical and writing faculties.

The Internet Movie Database (IMDB) at *www.imdb.com* is a good source of reviews of specific films. There are links to professional, published reviews of each film, as well as reviews posted by individuals wanting to share their thoughts (called, on the site, 'User Reviews'). It's a good way to compare and contrast the thoughts of the critics and the general public.

National Non-fiction Day

National Non-fiction Day is an annual celebration, initiated in the UK by the Federation of Children's Book Groups, in partnership with Scholastic Children's Books. It aims to celebrate all that is brilliant about non-fiction and show that it's not just fiction that can be read and enjoyed for pleasure.

The first National Non-fiction Day was celebrated in November 2010, and it will take place annually thereafter on the first Thursday in November.

The event offers opportunities to tie in specific non-fiction writing activities.

✓ Why not ask the children to keep a non-fiction diary for the day: not writing about how they felt, but just detailing what happened during the day. But they still need to make sure it's an interesting read.

✓ Or ask the children to write non-fiction riddle cards: each child chooses to be an animal or object for the day. They then write a card listing a few cryptic facts about their creature/object. The challenge for the other children is to work out who, or what, they are – based on this information.

✓ With a little thought, the possibilities are endless.

The National Non-fiction Day website is at *http://nnfd.org*. It aims to give children as much information as possible about National Non-fiction Day, as well as information about non-fiction titles, authors and available resources, to be used in the classroom or at home.

5 Writing with Digital Tools

5 Writing with Digital Tools

 The Issues

 Digital tools and digital technologies

Until recently the term 'information technology' (IT), or 'information and communication technology' (ICT), referred to desktop computers (usually allied to the resources of the Internet). Even now, ICT lessons in schools are all-too-often (sadly) limited to working with Powerpoint, Word, Excel and web browsers on the ubiquitous PC.

But digital technologies have moved on – and will continue to do so.

Any discussion of digital technologies to be used in writing must now include mobile phones, smartphones and tablet computers (such as the iPad).

We must also be ready and willing to make use of new devices and new tools (where they can help us) as they become available.

Many children are now growing up with mobile digital devices of their own. They may have smartphones and portable games consoles, for example. This makes for a much closer relationship between the child and the technology than in the past, when children were using only laptops or desktop computers.

Of course there's nothing new about using technology in writing. In fact, it's virtually impossible to write without using some kind of technology – whether it be pen and paper, Chinese inkstones and brushes or Babylonian cuneiform tablets that are baked in the oven.

The keyboard as a writing tool

Computers and keyboards (of various kinds) are now part of everyday life. Most professional writers use them and, with some exceptions, they have become essential tools of the writing trade.

So children need to learn how to make the best use of these tools. After all, the tools are *useful* – and anyway, once they are adults the children will use these tools in employment and in their daily lives.

Of course, children need also to develop their handwriting skills. It's not a case of either/or. It's *both* handwriting *and* keyboard skills.

The benefit of work that has been typed in – that is held *digitally* – is that it can easily be manipulated, or edited. It can also be transferred or copied.

Composing at the keyboard

We are all aware of the benefits of typing a creative work (such as an important letter) rather than writing it out by hand. We can revisit the text on the screen at any time, adding words and moving passages around until we are happy with it. With pen and paper, we would need to start again each time we wished to change something.

Similarly, it is much easier for children to edit their work if it's on a computer than if it's handwritten. This does, however, require a different approach to the task.

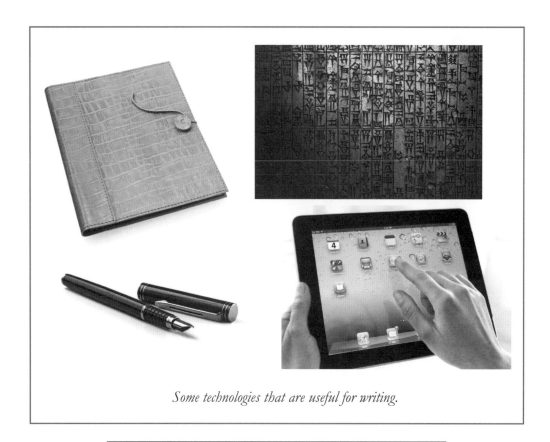

Some technologies that are useful for writing.

 When children undertake a creative writing task using pen and paper, they will usually need to work out exactly what they intend to write before commencing the writing task. On the computer, they can sketch out notes – gradually expanding them into a completed text.

You, as the supervising adult (or teacher), can edit the text on screen with the child. You don't need a red pen and the child can see their work improving as you work on it together, rather than having it 'marked' as a separate process.

There is, however, absolutely no point in a child writing something on paper with a pen and then laboriously copying it onto the computer. That's enough to put any child off writing for life. Discourage it strongly.

The trick is to encourage the children to think at the keyboard, letting their fingers become the pen. That means they type as the ideas flow – in just the same way that I'm writing this book. The words are appearing on my computer screen almost as quickly as they form in my mind. I have a few handwritten notes – headings and book titles and so on – in a notebook at my side, but otherwise I'm 'composing at the keyboard'.

 With encouragement, children at Key Stages 1 and 2 (ages 5 – 11) will adapt to working in this way very quickly, especially if the school also teaches touch typing so that the children are quick and accurate on the keyboard.

By the time they get to Key Stage 3 (aged 12), typing on a keyboard should be second nature.

The advantages of the keyboard

Some of the advantages of writing with the keyboard are that the young writer can:

✓ move words, sentences and paragraphs around

✓ consult the computer's dictionary or thesaurus (but make sure the setting is for your region's spelling (e.g. UK, not US, English)

✓ use the grammar check

✓ use the spellcheck (again, set for local spellings), although as you help the young writers be aware that computer spellcheckers are not foolproof. They will sometimes 'correct' a word into one which isn't what the writer intended – often with hilarious results. It's useful for checking typing errors, though

✓ link literacy activities with curriculum ICT work

✓ easily get facts needed to inform the writing (by consulting the Internet and/or other resources at the same time)

✓ often work more quickly (many pupils can type faster than they can write with a pen)

✓ save the work (whether completed or not) and readily return to it later

✓ produce very neat, professional-looking work which is satisfying and good for the child's self-esteem.

Students with a specific learning difficulty such as dyslexia usually benefit from working with a keyboard. That is why, for public exams such as GCSE and A level, schools can get special dispensation for students with learning difficulties to write their answers on computers rather than by hand.

Some children write better quality stories, poems and other forms of creative writing using a computer than they ever would with pen and paper. For reasons it's hard to pin down, technology seems to liberate creativity for some people.

Copying digital text

Anything a child has typed in on a computer or portable device, such as a smartphone or tablet, can then be re-presented in a variety of ways. It could be:

- read on a computer screen
- projected onto an electronic white board
- emailed (e.g. to a newspaper or to a friend)
- posted on the school intranet or on a blog
- incorporated into a digital presentation (e.g. in Powerpoint or similar), or
- just printed out.

It always pays to think about how a child's creative work can best be presented (to the satisfaction of both the child and the intended audience), once it is in a digital format.

> **I**t is tremendously rewarding for a child to see their work presented 'professionally' – with a good choice of fonts, set margins and a clean layout.

 ## Are computers always best?

A study published in 2011, led by reading specialist Professor Anne Mangen of The University of Stavanger in Norway, suggested that children and students who write by hand learn more effectively than those who type.

In Professor Mangen's view, when an individual is writing by hand the brain receives feedback from the muscles and fingertips. This kind of feedback is stronger than feedback received by typing on a keyboard, and this, it is argued, strengthens the learning mechanism.

> The message of this study may be that if we want children to learn facts, methods, theories and so on through note-taking, then handwriting may be better.

Since writing by hand takes longer than writing on a keyboard, the additional time devoted to the task may also positively influence the learning process.

There seems, however, to be no suggestion in Mangen's study that keyboard use in any way inhibits the creativity needed for other forms of writing which are original to the writer.

More information about Mangen's work can be found on the University of Stavanger website at *www.uis.no/news/article29782-50.html*.

Certainly, it seems to be the case that a writer who is using a computer will approach the task in a different way from a writer using traditional pen and paper. Indeed, some (admittedly older) authors still write their books in 'longhand', before getting them typed up on the computer. I am, however, not entirely sure what conclusions we can draw from this.

Making the most of developing technologies

Technologies change so quickly that anything written about them tends to be out of date almost before the ink is dry. Remember video tapes, laser discs, fax machines, cassette tapes and polaroid cameras? None seemed to be with us for long before being superseded by something 'better' (or, at least, different).

 There's limited value, therefore, in listing ways in which specific technologies can be used to engage children as writers. Nevertheless, I have detailed some in the second half of this chapter, as examples.

There are two key things to hold on to here, I think. The first is that we need constantly to be aware of how new and emerging technologies can be used to support writing. The trick is to think imaginatively:

'How can I use this to help the children to write – and to write well?'

The second point can be a little more tricky to manage, especially in a teaching environment:

Give the children the freedom to use the technology in (almost) any way they want to.

Children have a habit of mastering this kind of technology and its potential very quickly, especially if they're allowed (and encouraged) to experiment. Often the children will become more adept with the tools than you are as the adult in charge. This is not in itself a bad thing. Although traditionally in a community knowledge resides with the oldest (and most experienced) members of that community, in the case of technology the opposite is often true: the younger you are (within reason), the more you know.

One boy's creative use of technology

A father I know recently sent me this email.

" *Our eldest is ten. He doesn't read or write much outside school. But over Christmas he was playing the FIFA football game on the Nintendo Wii. He created little dramas featuring famous players – a foul, an awful miss – and created them on the Wii, replayed with a 3D rotate (don't ask me how).*

Next he'd write a commentary to go with it. Then he'd replay the Wii recording, video-recording it on his smartphone while narrating his commentary over the top. This was saved to the phone as a movie, bluetoothed to my Mac and uploaded to a dedicated channel he created on YouTube. He then used the school newsgroup email facility to tell all his mates, so they'd go online to see it.

He's done fifteen of these movies (so far). I'd say that's a pretty good use of common or garden technology to get tech savvy boys creating their own narratives ... "

Well yes, I agree so wholeheartedly that I have little to add, which is why I have reproduced the email in full.

The message for teachers and parents, I think, is to give children and young people their heads, never underestimate their creativity and accept that there are almost as many ways of unlocking the writer in every child as there are children.

Learn with the children and learn from the children. Don't ever allow your own nervousness, ineptitude or lack of knowledge hold the children back.

Some findings about children's writing and technology

In 2008 the UK's National Literacy Trust, in partnership with the UK charity Booktrust, carried out a survey to find out more about UK children's attitudes towards writing. Over 3,000 children and young people were questioned and the results were published in 2009.

Amongst other things the study discovered that:

Writing and digital technology

✓ 75% of young people said that they write regularly.

✓ Digital technology-based formats were the most popular form for writing:

- 82% of young people wrote text messages at least once a month
- 73% wrote instant messages (such as messages on AIM, Blackberry IM or MSN)
- 63% wrote on a social networking site at least once a month.

✓ Of non-technology-based writing, 77% wrote notes or answers in class or for homework at least once a month (which raises the question – what did the others do?), with 52% writing notes to other people.

Social networking and blogs

✓ 56% of young people said they had a profile on a social networking site such as Bebo or Facebook.

✓ 24% said that they had their own blog.

To quote from the report:

"While frequently vilified in the media as 'dumbing down' young people's literacy, this research shows that technology offers different writing opportunities for young people, which is seen in a link between blogging and (self-reported) writing ability and enjoyment of writing. For example, young people who write on a blog were much more likely than young people who do not write on a blog to enjoy writing in general (57% vs. 40%) and to enjoy writing for family/friends in particular (79% vs. 55%). Young people with a blog (61%) as well as young people with a profile on a social networking site (56%) also displayed greater confidence, believing themselves to be good writers. Blog owners and young people with a social networking profile were also more prolific writers than their counterparts. They held more positive attitudes towards writing and computer use, and viewed writers more favourably."

(*Young People's Writing, Attitudes, Behaviour and the Role of Technology*, Christina Clark and George Dugdale, Executive summary, November 2009. © National Literacy Trust.)

The full report can be found at *www.literacytrust.org.uk/research/nlt_research /261_young_peoples_writing_attitudes_behaviour_and_the_role_of_technology*.

5 Writing with Digital Tools

Practical Teaching Ideas

 ## Working with the youngest children

Here are two approaches for using computers with the youngest children.

 ### First steps on a computer

✎ Young children see using a computer as a very grown-up activity, and it helps to makes the business of writing appealing to the youngest children – those (in the UK) at Foundation Stage or at the beginning of Key Stage 1 (ages 5 – 6).

✎ Using a computer in this way can make the child aware of a form of writing which needs different sorts of motor and eye skills from handwriting. With older children, you are also reinforcing the links between upper and lower case letters. Moreover, this activity is the very beginning of familiarisation with the QWERTY keyboard – an essential life skill.

Netbooks and touch tablets are a useful resource for very young children if the school can run to them, because the smaller keyboard is ideal for small hands. It's also easier to position it on a desk, a table or a lap at the right height for very young children.

 Set the computer to display a clear font and large point size. On the computer screen (unlike on paper) sans serif fonts are best (i.e. 'this' rather than 'this').

 Sit down with the child at the computer. Show him or her where the initial letter is for his or her name and let the child type it.

> Try to use a font with letter shapes that match the letter shapes the children are learning at school – a and g are the usual letters to watch. **Comic sans** is a popular (if overused) font. **Sassoon** is another favourite.

 Work up to typing the child's whole name – and, in time, other things such as a sentence of news, a simple story or anything else the child wants to write.

> A very useful piece of learning from this activity is that the letters displayed on the QWERTY keyboard itself are upper case, but when you type them (unless you engage the caps lock key) they appear as lower case. So the child can immediately see the connection.

 Writing first emails

Writing and sending emails is another very 'grown-up' activity and an important way of communicating in the 21st century. And it's something else which cannot be introduced too early.

I would introduce email at Foundation Stage, if possible.

 If you are able to give each child a safe, controlled email address of their own, then do so. Otherwise use your own or one belonging to the centre or school – sending the child's message as an attachment.

 Get each child to think of someone to whom they would like to send a message. It could be Mum, Dad, a sibling or a friend at the school.

 Type the recipient's address for the child and 'Message from Evie' (or Archie or whomever) in the title box. Then help the child to type his or her name and some kisses. Use a big, clear font. Then send the message.

> You may need to organise this in advance the first time you do it, so that you have the relevant email address(es) to hand.

✒ You should very soon be able to take this further. Get the children to write more than just their names – perhaps a sentence about what they have been doing today. Or together you could find and attach an emoticon or picture to send.

As an alternative, you could also show the children how to write very simple text messages on a mobile phone.

Social networking

Whether you 'get it' or not, social networking is now part of the fabric of communication. Young adults make extensive use of it – and it offers great opportunities for writing.

Twitter

✒ Twitter (*http://twitter.com*) is a good medium for reluctant writers because each message (they are known as 'tweets') is limited to 140 characters, including spaces. Twitter is often called a 'microblogging site'.

> The site could appeal especially to boys who are turned off by large, empty screens or blank sheets of paper.

✒ In 2010 the production company Mudlark, together with the Royal Shakespeare Company, ran a project called *Such Tweet Sorrow*, whereby six characters unfolded a modern, very upbeat version of Romeo and Juliet in the form of Twitter messages sent to each other and to the thousands of people who followed it.

 Here are some ideas for using Twitter in class.

✓ Get a group to make up a story by contributing one or two sentences each as they go along, publishing them on Twitter. Each contributor responds to what has gone before.

✓ Encourage a group, in the same way, to invent a modern continuation of a well-known story such as Cinderella and tell it, sentence by sentence, on Twitter.

> They could do this in the third person (using the pronouns 'he' and 'she', or they could take on the roles of the characters in the story, using 'I' or 'we'.

✓ Take turns to comment on current events, sport and the media – such as those reported on the BBC website (*www.bbc.co.uk*).

✓ Or you could set a task of telling a complete story in 140 characters – i.e. in a single tweet. Decide whether or not to allow text-style language and other abbreviations. This is quite a challenge activity, but it is good fun. Here are two examples:

Pushy Jack met happy Chloe at Olly's party. They gazed, talked, drank, danced, kissed, quarrelled and parted. Both cried later.

(127 characters)

OUT bullied, sad Cinders 2 ball 'cos F'y G'mother owes favour. Falls 4 prince but has 2 leave fast. He finds her & shoe fits. They marry HEA

(140 characters)

I've coined Elkin text-speak in the second example above: OUT for 'Once upon a time' and HEA for 'Happy ever after'. Notice that I had to omit the final full stop to keep the tweet to 140 characters.

✓ Get the children to write their own tweets and to be as imaginative as they like. It can work well as long as you make sure that the readers understand the 'code'.

Facebook

✎ Facebook has exploded amongst teens and young adults, as they discover the benefits of social networking in their tens of thousands. As blogger Mia Freedman put it:

> 'Whether you like it or not, hanging out virtually on Facebook has replaced hanging out in the street, like we used to do. And it's pointless to fight it.'

✎ Stephen Heppell, Professor of New Media Environments at Bournemouth University (*www.heppell.net*), has suggested that teachers should set up separate Facebook pages for their teacher presence. This page/account should be quite separate from any personal Facebook pages.

✎ Heppell suggests that the teachers call themselves something related to the subject they teach – such as 'Geography Steve', or that they use another form of 'Miss' (such as Missy), as Facebook doesn't allow 'Mr' or 'Mrs' titles.

Although Facebook generally frowns on users creating two accounts, it has actively encouraged teachers who have wanted to do it, according to Professor Heppell.

✏ Teachers setting up Facebook accounts should not befriend pupils, Heppell advises. Rather, they should allow the children to take the initiative. They should not read their pupils' Facebook pages and should never chat via instant message.

✏ But for giving children reminders about things such as impending exams, offering a space for informal chats outside of the traditional school environment and allowing parents and children to keep up with school news at a time and place that suits them, Facebook is invaluable, thinks Heppell.

✏ Facebook also has potential as a way of encouraging children and young people to share thoughts, such as their responses to current events, comments on books read, films and TV programmes seen, opinions, ideas, questions – and of course to tell stories.

⚙ Club Penguin

✏ Many younger children are keen members of Disney's Club Penguin, at *http://clubpenguin.com*. The site allows each child to take the role of a penguin avatar in a virtual world for kids – and it prides itself on its online safety. In many ways Club Penguin is a carefully controlled social networking site, since the children are able to send each other messages, etc.

✏ In addition, since children can invent narratives by playing Club Penguin games such as Card-Jitsu Fire, there is scope for some writing activities here.

⚙ Blogging

✏ Blogging is an excellent writing opportunity, since it mostly requires – writing. It's also more attractive to many children and young adults than writing with pen and paper. Blogs have the advantage of being quick and easy to update, and the children's blogs are immediately available to a large audience.

In addition, since the blog is more than a simple collection of written pieces, it's easy to create a sustained narrative, encouraging both bloggers and their readers to return. That in turn generates a habit of blogging – i.e. writing.

Radiowaves

Radiowaves (*www.radiowaves.co.uk/class*) is a schools-based network which works with 13,000 schools in 22 countries. The platform allows for images, audio, video, blogs and podcasts to be uploaded and shared, either just within the school, with other schools on the Radiowaves network or with the larger world, including parents. And the emphasis is firmly on children's safety in the potentially dangerous world of social networking.

At Bedford Primary School in Liverpool, for example, children interview, record and photograph many aspects of school life for inclusion on the site. In 2011 the British Council funded four pupils from Bedford Primary School to visit schools in China. Every moment of the trip was recorded in a video diary and viewed back in Liverpool – via Radiowaves.

> The site has attracted the attention of the British Council, which has seen the potential for forging real and long-lasting links with schools around the world. And a lot of this linking, inevitably – like all social networking – involves writing.

Voki

Voki is a free web-based service that allows anyone to create personalized speaking avatars, or computer-generated characters, and use them on their blogs, profiles, and in email messages, etc. The website is at *www.voki.com*.

✐ Voki has now launched a dedicated education site with lots of possibilities for creative writing:

✓ Pupils could create their own avatars and keep a journal, either recording their own voices or using text to speech applications.

✓ Or you could create a Voki and start to tell a story – which the pupils are then invited to finish.

✓ If you have a class blog or website, you could create a Voki and use it to welcome readers/visitors.

✓ Children could pretend to be newsreaders and report news as Vokis.

✐ Voki has two dedicated, experienced, educationalists working on ideas such as these. It's worth signing up to receive their regular e-newsletter.

 # Motivating reluctant writers

Now to some ideas for motivating children who can already write but who may not want to, and could certainly do it better.

 ## Myst

✐ *Myst* – the word is a fusion of 'mist' and 'mystery' – is a graphic adventure computer game designed and directed by the brothers Robyn and Rand Miller. It was first released in 1993 and has achieved great success, with versions available for a range of platforms, including Microsoft Windows (PC) and Xbox, Sony PlayStation and PSP, Nintendo DS, and the Apple iOS. There have also been a number of sequels.

✐ *Myst* puts the player in the role of the Stranger, who uses a special book to travel to the island of Myst. There, the player uses other special books written by an artisan and explorer named Atrus in order to travel to several worlds known as 'Ages'. Clues found in each of these Ages help reveal the back-story of the game's characters. The game has several endings, depending on the course of action the player takes.

✐ The open structure of the game makes it ideal to inspire children's creative confidence in many areas of the curriculum, including creative writing, speaking and listening, music and art. The ex-teacher Tim Rylands (*www.timrylands.com*) has achieved considerable success in this regard, particularly using *Myst*. His inspirational website contains plenty of ideas and suggestions.

> Similar approaches could be taken with other popular video and computer game formats.

 ## Five card Flickr

✐ Based on a card game, this website states that it is designed to foster visual thinking, but in fact it is also a powerful tool to foster creative writing.

✐ The website contains a database of photographs. The 'player' is dealt five random photos for each draw and is invited to choose one each time to add to a selection of images. Taken together, the five selected images tell a story in pictures.

✐ The player is required to tell the story illustrated by the pictures, and is given the option of adding a title and explanation. The finished work can be saved so that it can be shared with others. The site also offers the ability to tweet the story or to use an embed code to add it to the player's (or school's) own website.

✐ The site is at *http://web.nmc.org/5cardstory/index.php*.

Storybird

✎ Storybird is a website (at *http://storybird.com*) designed to promote collaborative storytelling. Storybirds are short, art-inspired stories which users of the site can make to share, read and print. As the website states: '*Read them like books, play them like games, and send them like greeting cards. They're curiously fun.*' There are some delightful examples of storybirds on the website.

✎ Teachers can create free class accounts to manage pupils who don't have individual email addresses. These accounts can also be used to create assignments and build thematic libraries based on the children's own stories. These can then be shared with parents and other schools.

✎ A very clear video on the Storybird website explains exactly how it all works.

Story Cubes

✎ As already mentioned on page 60, Rory's Story Cubes are a simple, low-tech idea to generate imaginative fiction. Story Cubes are a set of nine dice-like cubes, each with six faces and each bearing a little picture.

 So there are 54 different pictures and over 10 million possible combinations. The child throws the nine dice and then creates a story from the nine pictures that the throw reveals.

✎ More information is available from *www.storycubes.com*. The Story Cubes are also available as an iOS app to use on the iPhone and iPad.

PicLits

- PicLits is an interesting website that aims to provide inspiration for writing short stories. It tries to accomplish this goal by providing users with images, around which they can build their writing. To get writers started, PicLits provides a list of words which can be dragged and dropped into sentence form. If you don't need a word list, you can select the 'freestyle' option to begin free-form writing.

- The idea of PicLits is not to write a full story within the images, but rather to use the images as the inspiration for longer pieces. Users of PicLits can create a free account in which to save their work.

- The website is at *www.piclits.com/compose_dragdrop.aspx*. There is a wealth of advice and free material for teachers on the site.

Some additional ideas

In-school training and support

- Bev Humphrey is a literacy, school libraries and technology consultant based in the UK. '*I have a passion for enthusing young people about reading and writing using new technologies,*' she says.

- She runs very dynamic workshops in schools along with teacher training, mentoring and other services. Bev, who is freelance, works with The Schools Network (formerly The Specialist Schools and Academies Trust) and Renaissance Learning, among other organisations.

- She can be contacted at *www.bevhumphrey.com*.

Alternative devices

Traditionally children have worked in schools with the conventional desktop computer, extending perhaps (where funds allow) to using laptop computers. However there is a range of other devices that could be used, funds and availability permitting.

The Neo 2

✓ The Neo 2 is a cheap, easy-to-use laptop computer (or 'notebook') designed especially for school use. It features a full-size keyboard, built-in spellchecker, thesaurus and typing tutor, and is designed to help pupils practise and establish essential touch-typing and writing skills and improve their overall standard of English. Built-in wireless technology is optimised for classroom use.

✓ The main attraction of the Neo2 is the price: it is available for around £150 at the time of writing, although bulk deals might reduce that price substantially.

✓ More information is available at *www.renlearn.co.uk/writing.*

Touch tablets and smartphones

✓ One of the key developments in technology in the past few years has been the emergence of a series of new 'platforms' – namely smartphones and touch tablets. In parallel with this development we have seen the arrival of so-called 'apps' for these devices, which can be downloaded (often for free) from a dedicated 'app store'.

✓ Many schools are now investing in touch tablets (such as the iPad or other devices running the Android operating system) rather than in laptop or netbook computers. The main feature of apps for these devices is that they are often relatively cheap to purchase (if not free) and they are regularly updated. At the time of writing, for example, the Apple appstore has over 425,000 apps for download.

✓ Not surprisingly, there is a good range of apps (both for Apple and for Android devices) that are engaging for young people and that can be used to support writing. Here are just a few:

> For younger children: *Intro to Letters* and *Alpha Writer*, both by Montessorium, *Pocketphonics Lite*, by Apps in My Pocket.
>
> Easy routes into writing: *SketchpadHD* (note-taking and sketching), *Noteshelf*, *Thinking Space* (mind mapping).
>
> For more accomplished writers: *Evernote*, *EasyWriter*, *Simplenote*, *SolidNote*, *mNote*.

✓ The list, of course, is almost endless. Of course the real fun is in finding game-like apps and subverting their purpose to support writing activities.

Happy hunting!

6 Working with Professional Writers

6 Working with Professional Writers

 The Issues

 Professional writers

Children and young people love meeting writers whose names they have seen in print or on websites.

So it's well worth inviting authors into school to talk to and work with your pupils. Such a visit often generates or inspires writing which pupils would not have thought of or attempted without meeting and/or working with the visitor.

Writers who are willing to run workshops and/or give talks in schools include:

- novelists
- poets
- playwrights
- journalists, including news reporters, critics, feature writers, columnists
- film screenplay writers
- adaptors of stories who convert, say, a novel into a script for a play or film, and
- writers of factual books for children.

Children get very excited about meeting authors – the names on the covers of books – and it is a powerful way of encouraging reading. Pupils will want to read some of the books before they meet a writer. Or, if they have already done so, they are motivated and curious to read the books after meeting him or her.

 Most authors bring copies of their books with them so that pupils (advised in advance to bring some money) can buy them and get them signed. Or you could invite parents along and let them do the buying.

Authors will usually sign copies of their books already owned by pupils or by the school.

How might a professional author help to unlock the writers inside my students?

A writer's workshop with students could include:

- brainstorming interesting/original words and expressions
- assembling words and ideas into poems
- games and exercises in collaborative story telling
- role play in pairs or groups, leading to a scripted playlet
- constructing an argument for or against a proposed development, such as a new local shopping centre
- putting together a short news article about an event (real or imagined) in school or nearby
- running a publishing workshop to explore the process of getting a book published.

Finding writers

You can approach writers by writing to their publisher. Publisher's contact details are printed at the front of all books. A quick Internet search will usually provide an email address for the publisher.

The National Association of Writers in Education (*www.nawe.co.uk*) has a directory on its website of authors who make school visits, and this might be the best place to start. The Society of Authors may also be able to help (*www.societyofauthors.net*).

> Some other useful websites are:
> - *www.ContactAnAuthor.co.uk*
> - *www.childrensdiscovery.org.uk/writers-in-schools*
> - *www.booktrust.org.uk/Resources-for-schools/Looking-for-an-author.*

You can also contact many authors via Twitter or Facebook.

 Some of the best author visits I have arranged have stemmed from my having heard the writer speaking well and entertainingly at teachers' courses and at conferences.

I've then buttonholed the author, or contacted him or her later, and negotiated a visit to my school. This has meant that I've been confident that the author is good at communicating orally.

Bear in mind that being able to write a fine novel or leader column in a newspaper does not necessarily make you good at inspiring young people. I have heard writers speaking in public who were orally so weak that I would not have dreamed of inviting them to work with my students.

That's something to find out *before* you invite him or her to visit.

If you want to contact a newspaper employee, a blogger or a professional journalist, look for an email address. Failing that, telephone the newspaper switchboard and ask if you can have the individual's email address. You might also ask for (and get) a direct line phone number, but be very wary of using this. Journalists are busy people, routinely expected to juggle many things at once and always working to tight, fixed deadlines. If you pick the wrong moment to phone you are likely to get very short shrift rather than an encouraging discussion about the possibility of a visit to your school.

 ## Structuring the writer's time

Try to book your author for a half or a whole day, so that he or she can run workshops with one or more groups of children.

Discuss beforehand with your writer what he or she plans to cover. If your focus is on writing, ensure that this will be the author's focus too. (A workshop on reading and evaluating texts, for example, will not go down well if a writing workshop was expected.)

In a workshop the writer will be focused on getting the children to write and on showing them new ways of generating ideas and developing them (by imaginative use of language) into stories, poems and other forms. A professional writer will usually role-model the creative process for the students, explaining how they work and making practical suggestions to help beginner writers.

 Alternatively, consider having a writer-in-residence. This means that the writer works with the school over a period of time – perhaps a term – during which they come into school on a number of occasions in order to build up some sustained writing work with the children.

From this there would normally be a larger-scale end-product, such as a collection of pupils' poems or a collaboratively written play which could be given a reading for parents and friends at the end of term.

What will it cost?

Most authors (and that includes novelists, playwrights and poets) are self-employed people, and so they will expect to charge for their time visiting schools.

So if this isn't part of your school budget, you have to find a way of paying for it. The school's Parent Teacher Association (PTA) might help, for instance, or there might be a local business which would be prepared to sponsor it.

You might be very lucky and persuade a staff journalist (one who is employed by their publication and therefore on salary) to come as a favour, without charging a fee. The journalist might then want to write about their experience in your school as a quid pro quo – a useful bonus for you in that it gets your school a bit of free positive publicity.

Remember, though, that many journalists now work on a freelance basis, which means they are likely to want to charge for their time, like other writers.

You are, realistically, unlikely to get a big name national journalist to come and work with your class, but your local paper may be willing to help.

There is a corollary, of course, however unappealing. If you are paying for an author to visit, you are much more likely to focus on getting value for money and ensuring that there are some real, useful outcomes for the children. Paying for a visit reduces the chances of it being treated as an afternoon's recreational diversion.

When you've got your author visit organised, don't forget to invite the local paper to take some pictures. Author visits are quite high profile and it will be a feather in your cap with the head if you can get some good, positive exposure for the school.

Virtual author visits

As an alternative to an author actually visiting your school, it might be possible to arrange a virtual author visit. This has the advantage that travel time (and travel costs) are eliminated.

There are a number of ways in which this could be done:

✓ a question and answer session or discussion, conducted over the Internet, using tools such as Skype (with a videolink) or simple Instant Messaging (IM) applications

✓ a Twitter chat with the author

✓ more ambitious writing workshops, again using Skype (or similar).

 The author Tommy Donbavand, for example, has run very successful writing workshops. His website (*http://www.tommydonbavand.com/author-visits/*) includes very useful information on how to make the most of an author visit – as well as what not to do.

6 Working with Professional Writers

Practical Teaching Ideas

Preparing for a visit from a novelist

It goes almost without saying that you should familiarise the students with some of the visiting novelist's books and stories.

- The students should know enough about the writer's output to be able to ask informed questions such as '*Where did you get the idea for* [e.g. Jack's] *character from?*'

- Ask the students to write some stories, poems, emails, letters, blog posts or anything else you or they can think of, based on or inspired by a character or situation in one of the writer's books.

- Any activity of this sort will help the students begin to think about how the writer works, so they will be well-placed to meet and work with him or her on the day.

For example the students might:

- write a new adventure for one of the writer's characters ('fan fiction')
- imagine and write what happens after the last page
- write a conversation (which could be via email, for example) between two characters about something which occurs in the book
- retell something which happens in the novel from the point of view of a different character, or
- write a monologue for one of the characters and then perform it.

 # Preparing for a visit from a poet

 Read some of the writer's poems to, or with, the class before the visit.

 Discuss whether there are any themes in the poet's work. Do they often write, for example, about animals, or school life or love?

 Poetry and prose

A bit of awareness-raising about the differences between poetry and prose could be useful too. Point out that poetry might:
- rhyme (or it might not)
- use devices such as alliteration
- be set out in shorter lines than continuous prose
- be arranged in verses (possibly of even or uneven length)
- use simple or complex language
- be short
- relate to none of the things on this list but still be poetry.

✏ If the children are not used to writing poetry, make sure they have all had a go before your visitor arrives. Ensure that the students bear in mind the above caveats about the defining features of poetry.

✏ The idea is that the children should be as informed as possible, so that they get maximum benefit from the visit.

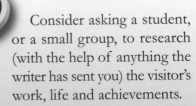

Consider asking a student, or a small group, to research (with the help of anything the writer has sent you) the visitor's work, life and achievements.

They could then summarise this in a short piece of writing which could form the basis of an oral introduction of the author to the class.

Preparing for a visit from a playwright or adaptor

✏ The children will probably be very aware of novelists, poets and playwrights as 'writers', but they may be less aware of the role of a writer who adapts a known work (such as a Harry Potter novel) for the stage or screen (whether for film or television).

✏ Spend some time with the children discussing the requirements of an adaptation of a novel. Considerations include:
  • fidelity to the original narrative (although sometimes film versions have simplified plots and even different endings)
  • the need to provide 'stage directions' as well as narration
  • the difficulty of getting the story across when there is no opportunity to explain what is happening (other than via the characters' dialogue).

Show the children part or all of a film adapted from a book that they know well. For example:

- *Goodnight Mister Tom* (1998), adapted by Brian Finch from Michelle Magorian's novel
- *The Railway Children* (1970), adapted by Lionel Jeffries from E Nesbit's novel, or
- *The Chronicles of Narnia: The Lion, the Witch and the Wardrobe* (2005), adapted by Ann Peacock, Andrew Adamson, Christopher Markus and Stephen McFeely from C. S. Lewis's novel.

There are many other possibilities.

Get the children to think about:
- ways in which the film version differs from its source novel
- why the adaptor made such changes.

Then, when they meet their own adaptor, they will know enough about the issues to ask thoughtful questions.

As an activity ask the children to choose an incident from a favourite story or novel and rework it as a playlet. They could do this in pairs or small groups and then give the script to another group to rehearse and perform to the class.

 # Preparing for a visit from a journalist

Use some class time to look at and discuss the publication the journalist works for, or one which regularly publishes his or her work.

Points to consider together:

- What sort of writing is this? Is it news, feature, opinion, a review or something else?
- Does the writer use long or short sentences?
- Is the vocabulary simple, complex or a combination?
- What sort of reader does the piece seem to be aimed at? Men? Women? Teachers? Office workers? Mothers at home? What is the likely age of the target reader? How can you tell?
- How has the writer researched their piece and how can you tell?

Prepare some questions to ask the writer.

Then get the pupils to have a go at writing something of their own, modelled on something the journalist has written.

 # After the author's visit

Thanks are called for. Ask the students to write letters or emails (in an imaginative format if they wish) to the visitor to thank him or her for the session(s).

Encourage the students to make comments about what they learned and the effect it has had on their own writing, rather than writing something generic and meaningless such as '*It was brilliant*' without giving any reasons.

Practical tips to ensure a successful author visit

- Establish clearly with the author beforehand
  - what he or she is proposing to do
  - the maximum number of children he or she will be happy to work with
  - how long the session(s) will be – and how these will be structured
  - what resources the author will require (e.g. photocopies, a whiteboard, microphone, etc.) and what the children will need.
- Send directions to the author about how to get to your school (and where to park) a few days in advance.
- Give the author a contact name and number in case they have a transport problem en route to your school.
- Ensure that all admin chores (e.g. payment of invoices, arrival and signing in, lunchtime arrangements, locations of toilets, etc.) are dealt with quickly, so that the day is as stress-free as possible.
- Discuss with the author whether he or she would be willing and able to bring copies of his or her books into school to sell, or whether you should order them yourself. This may need some advance preparation. If the author will be selling books on the day, you might want to send out letters to parents so that the children can bring in money for this purpose. You may also consider taking orders in advance.
- Make sure your school library has copies of the author's books for children to enjoy. It's also worth informing local bookshops and the local media of the visit. An author visit is something to be celebrated.
- Organise time in the day for book signing, if you want it to be part of the event.
- Let the author know if any children with special needs have particular requirements.
- Make sure you discuss with the author in advance any extra things you'd like him or her to do – e.g. giving out prizes, opening a new library, etc.
- Plan the day so that the rooms used for the workshops will be as quiet as possible.

7 Publishing Children's Work

7 Publishing Children's Work

 The Issues

 Opportunities to publish

It gives children's writing a lot of status if you can find ways of making their work public and sharing it with a wider audience.

In this context therefore 'publishing' really means making the child's (or student's) work available for others to see and read. This could be as simple as putting it up on the classroom wall, or it could extend to making the work available as part of a professionally published book.

 We have already discussed (in Chapter 4) posting reviews of Carnegie Medal shortlisted books on the CILIP – Chartered Institute of Librarians and Information Professionals – website. We also looked at Storybird, a means of sharing children's stories, in Chapter 5.

Other ways of making children's work accessible to more people include:

Within school

- ✓ class or school anthologies of original work – whether paper-based or digital

- ✓ using sections of the school's intranet to display children's writing

- ✓ putting work on noticeboards and walls around the school

- ✓ getting children to read their work aloud to others in class and in assemblies.

On the Internet

- ✓ using sections of the school's website to display children's writing

- ✓ writing a class blog via a blogging site

- ✓ *www.cyberkids.com* and *www.cyberteens.com* are two reputable American sites looking for children's stories, articles and poems to publish.

'Professional' publication

- ✓ encouraging the children to write to newspapers and magazines, in the hope that their contribution might be published (see Chapter 5)

- ✓ creating a school or class yearbook, properly laid out (using desktop publishing software) and professionally printed. This could contain the group's best work, and at the end of the year each child could be given a copy as a memento of that year.

If the idea of creating a school or class yearbook as a vehicle for publishing students' writing appeals to you, try *www.myphotographics. co.uk*, which allows you to do most of the design work yourself, thereby keeping costs down – although it is still not cheap.

As an alternative, you could try to find a willing parent with the necessary layout skills.

 Lily, 8, recently spent part of half term with us. And she brought her homework with her. Her task was to make a poster showing the three times table. We suggested that she design it first before transferring the work to a sheet of A3 paper. She applied herself long and hard and ended up with an attractive, carefully done poster which included both numbers and words.

When I told her I thought she'd done well, her eyes shone. '*Perhaps Mrs Walker will display it in the Green Zone*' she said in excitement, referring to a section of the classroom wall reserved for children's best work.

It was a good lesson, for us as adults, in the motivational power of publishing pupil's work.

Choosing work to publish

Having your work chosen for publication should be an indication that the work is, in some way, special.

If you routinely publish the entire class's efforts it loses its cachet as a distinction to aim for. So be selective.

Look for work which:

✓ stands out for its originality

✓ is of high quality

✓ shows painstaking effort

✓ is an important achievement for a child who struggles, and/or

✓ is a real improvement for an individual child.

Remember that sometimes you are rewarding the effort that was put in, rather than the quality of the final work.

 ## Group writing

You might also want to publish collaborative work from a group or even from the whole class.

Collaborative work often achieves a much higher quality than contributing individuals would manage on their own.

When I was a Year 9 pupil (although we called it something else then) we studied the introduction to Dylan Thomas' *Under Milk Wood*. The teacher then asked us each to try writing a short passage of our own about an imaginary town or village waking up, using Thomas's style.

Two pupils were then sent off as editors to prepare a class composite version, using the best elements from each pupil's work. Several sentences of mine were included, although the only fragment I recall is *'The silent sun slides up the sky'*. Two or three students with dramatic bent then recorded the work, which was later played in assembly.

If you did this today you could easily produce a good quality recording, a copy of which could be given to every pupil. So it could be published much more widely.

I mention this here because it was a good example of group writing leading to a finished, quasi-published product of which we were all proud. And – like all the best things which happen in schools – I can remember it with great clarity many years later.

Presentation

I feel very strongly that work which contains spelling, punctuation and other errors should not be published in its 'raw' form.

It looks sloppy and careless, gives a poor impression of your pupils' (and your) standards to outsiders and – most worrying of all – perpetuates the error for other students who read the work.

We shall come on to the whole question of orthography – observing the conventions of spelling, grammar and punctuation – and how it fits into the world of unlocking young writers in the next chapter. Meanwhile, make sure that student's work is scrupulously proof-read before it is published in any form.

✓ In the first instance I would ask writers to check their own work.

✓ Then ask another child to check it. This is a good way of helping to make children aware of conventions and errors.

✓ But it also needs to be proof-read by a competent adult who, ideally, discusses the errors with the child so that he or she learns from the process.

All of this, of course, takes place *after* the young writer has composed their piece.

It isn't helpful to stress presentation conventions too strongly when a child is concentrating on creating something interesting or original. However, the ultimate aim is that the child will eventually be able to compose and manage orthography effortlessly at the same time, because the conventions are securely embedded. But that can take many years to achieve.

It is – obviously – much easier to draft and make changes to a document held digitally than one that has been written out by hand.

It is off-puttingly boring, and arguably a waste of time, for pupils to copy a piece of writing out several times.

> A tip: proof-reading a document on the computer screen is more likely to lead to errors being missed than if the document is printed out and the hard copy proof-read. It's to do with screen 'glare' and the generally low resolution of the computer screen.

Copyright

By law you may not publish someone else's work without the copyright holder's permission. The copyright – the right to copy – in a piece of writing usually belongs to the writer, although it may have been assigned elsewhere (e.g. to a publisher).

Children need to be re-minded of this frequently and they are never too young for you to start getting this message across. Children must not be allowed – easy as it is to do and difficult as it is to police – to steal (yes, *steal*) other people's work from the Internet. This applies whether they try to pass it off as their own or not.

One way of driving home this message is to insist that they use the copyright symbol with their name on every piece of work they produce (e.g. © Susan Elkin), until it becomes second nature.

This helps to encourage children to put a value on their own work and to take it seriously too.

You should also make a point of asking the young writer's permission before you publish or distribute their work to anyone else in any form.

Make sure that others hear you asking. You are very unlikely to be refused permission: most children are delighted when an adult is sufficiently pleased with their work that it is deemed worthy of sharing with others. In the unlikely event of a refusal, however, you must – of course – respect the pupil's wishes. This is a copyright matter and we are not just paying lip service to the law.

Copyright education

There are two free-to-download education packs, one for UK Key Stage 2 and one for Key Stage 3, on the Authors' Licensing and Collecting Society (ALCS) website. I wrote these packs for ALCS. They are designed to support teachers in educating students about copyright and include plenty of awareness-raising classroom activities. You will find them at *www.alcs.co.uk/Authors--rights/Copyright-education*.

> Some of the children whose inner writer we are currently unlocking will one day be paid, published authors in need of the services of ALCS to collect secondary use royalty payments on their behalf.

 ALCS, incidentally, is an important, independent UK-based organisation which protects the rights of authors' writing in all disciplines and ensures that writers receive fair payment for the various uses of their work.

7 Publishing Children's Work

Practical Teaching Ideas

Reviews on websites

Some websites offer very good opportunities for children to place considered reviews of books they have read or films they have seen, etc. Here are two such sites.

 Amazon

 Anyone can post a review on the Amazon website. Reviews are actually read by individuals considering purchasing the book or film in question, and it is rewarding for the children to know that their views are actually being taken into account.

 Placing reviews is best done on your national Amazon website (e.g. in the UK on *www.amazon.co.uk* rather than on *www.amazon.com*).

Encourage the children to write about the books (or films) that they've read or seen and that they have a view about – irrespective of whether that view is positive or negative. Give some classroom time to helping to refine these reviews, so that they say something really pertinent about the book or film and are presented as well as possible.

> Note that, unlike the IMDB site (below), Amazon is essentially a shopping website. Visitors are likely therefore to read a review with a view to deciding whether to purchase the book or film, or not. The children's reviews are therefore likely to be most useful if they take this into account.

IMDB

The Internet Movie Database (*www.imdb.com*) also contains user-posted reviews of films.

Again, this offers a good opportunity for the children to post reviews of films that they have seen and that they have views about.

Since the site also contains reviews of the films by professional critics, there are opportunities to compare the childrens' reviews with those of the critics. Some children might like to write a review of the critics' reviews, for example.

Note: it is probably better in all cases – for child protection reasons – for the children to use pseudonyms and to write and post their reviews only under supervision.

IMDB has also produced 'app' versions of the movie database for most smartphone and touchpad formats. Details are on its website.

Correspondence with fictional characters

◢ This activity can usefully be undertaken, with modifications, with any children aged around 7 or older.

◢ For younger children, choose a character in a fairy story – such as Goldilocks, Hansel or Rapunzel. Ask the children to write a letter (or email) to the fairytale character. The letter could comment on things which happened in the story, it could make comments or suggestions (e.g. suggesting to Goldilocks what she should have done) or it could just ask questions.

◢ Once completed, you could make a wall display with the children, with a large illustration of the character at the centre. Mount carefully proof-read fair copies of the children's letters around the edge.

> If working with emails, you could collect them together and publish them on the school's intranet, below a picture of the character.

◢ Older students could do something similar with characters from texts they are studying, or from favourite books (e.g. Lady Macbeth, Michael from *Kensuke's Kingdom* or Atticus Finch from *To Kill a Mockingbird*).

You could also use this technique to generate writing through current events awareness teaching.

'*What would you like to say to or ask ...* [e.g. the President of the United States, or the British Prime Minister]*?*

Variants of the Under Milk Wood idea

✎ Try getting Key Stage 3 students (aged 11 – 14) to create, in a group, their own *Under Milk Wood*-style recorded play – as I did when I was at school (see page 175).

✎ Alternatively, you could try some of these possibilities:

✓ Read all (or part) of Coleridge's balladic poem *The Rime of the Ancient Mariner.* Then ask the children to write a few verses in the same pattern about a topic of their choice, such as everyday school life. Get some pupils to edit and create a composite group poem assembled from the best verses. This could then be recorded – thereby including some useful speaking and listening work as an incidental.

For older students, collaborative writing can be a very creative activity.

✓ Read *The Mad Hatter's tea party* section of the book *Alice's Adventures in Wonderland*, in which characters keep saying odd things which don't relate to each other. It's a gloriously dysfunctional conversation. Ask the children to imagine a modern situation in which three or four unlikely people are trying (and failing) to talk each other. If each child writes a few 'wacky' sentences, the best of these could then be collated into a group effort for recording.

✓ Look at T. S. Eliot's poem *The Naming of Cats*. Set the children a group task of writing a poem called 'The Naming of Dogs' (or mice, horses, gerbils, etc.). This too, when edited and collated, works well as a recording – and you can use as many voices as you like.

Collaborative class blog

Creating a collaborative class blog is an activity that you can do at almost any age and stage, and it's easy to make it very inclusive.

✐ For the youngest children it could be simply a written electronic version of circle time or news sharing. Just ask each child to contribute a sentence or two – something that they really want to say, such as *'My rabbit, Jemima, has had four babies,'* or *'I'm worried about my Nan who's in hospital,'* or *'Sausages for lunch today. Yum yum.'* Around thirty of these sentences will give a real picture of the personalities that make up the class and their current preoccupations.

✐ Older students could make a statement – or ask a question – or say something insouciant about current events, their thoughts and feelings, what's worrying them and so on. This could then be assembled into a 'snapshot' of the class at a moment in time.

There's also scope here, of course, for an account of what the class has been doing, ongoing projects and so on.

8 And so to Orthography

_...n g...
...swers ca..._

...is the play Macbeth...

...classic tragedy because it...

...real old too. That's wat makes

_04_

8 And so to Orthography

 The Issues

 ## How important are spelling and grammar?

When we talk about children's writing many, if not most, people think immediately of spelling, punctuation, grammar, and legible, comfortable handwriting – rather than of the creative process which is what most of this book has been about.

And that attitude is not surprising.

 Orthography – which comes from the Greek words for 'correct' and for 'writing' – simply means a writing system. It is often used to mean just spelling, but in its widest sense the term covers all the conventions of writing within a 'system' which can be understood by others.

In this chapter I am using 'orthography' as an umbrella term to include the conventions of spelling, punctuation and grammar, along with some thoughts about handwriting.

Children who are struggling with the mechanical details – and who are being made very aware of their problems – tend to get bogged down, so that they *won't* or *can't* write imaginatively.

> To put it another way, that inner writer (which, I believe, lives in every child) stays firmly locked in.

A useful sanity check

At the time of writing (2011) the UK National Curriculum (UKNC) is under review, and is likely to be revised or replaced. That review notwithstanding, the UKNC requirements for English at Key Stages 1 and 2, in the section on writing, offer a good overview of the skills children need to be acquiring.

At Key Stages 1 and 2, 'composition' is treated as one small part of what needs to be covered, with equal emphasis given to spelling, punctuation and handwriting/presentation.

> For this reason these requirements are a good 'sanity check', a way of ensuring that children's orthographic skills are developing in a suitably rounded way.

Even at Key Stage 3, as well as a good list of all the creative things pupils should be encouraged to do, the National Curriculum specifies they must also study '*the principles of sentence grammar and whole-text cohesion* [see panel, next page], *and the use of this knowledge in pupils' writing.*'

Not that I have much quarrel with any of this.

> The more children and young people understand about how their language works, the better – in my experience – they are likely to use that language in their writing.

'The principles of sentence grammar and whole-text cohesion'

'The principles of sentence grammar and whole-text cohesion' are supposed to include, for Key Stage 3 (ages 11 – 14):

- word classes and their grammatical functions

- the structure of phrases and clauses and how they can be combined to make complex sentences (eg through co-ordination and subordination)

- paragraph structure and how to form different paragraphs

- the structure of whole texts, including cohesion, openings and conclusions in different types of writing (e.g. through the use of verb tenses and reference chains)

- the use of appropriate grammatical terminology to reflect on the meaning and clarity of individual sentences.

We also have – of course – a responsibility to teach children how to write in such a way that their ideas can be readily understood by others. That is, after all, what communication is all about.

And that means spelling accurately, using punctuation to support meaning and following the language's grammar conventions.

In other words – unless you want to create the breathy effect that Margaret Atwood did for the first-person narrator in her novel *Cat's Eye* – you must learn, for example, to end sentences with full stops rather than the comma.

Similarly, it is not acceptable to write 'I brung' or 'I bringed' instead of 'I brought', without a very good reason (such as the reason for writing it here).

Writing: conventions or rules?

Teachers and examiners speak gently and liberally of 'conventions' and 'appropriate use'. College admissions tutors, employers, media commentators and, to a large extent, the general public are more inclined to call spades 'spades'. They will readily use more direct and judgmental vocabulary to describe what they see as 'errors', 'bad grammar', 'weak spelling' and so on.

ince we have to educate young people to write in ways which fit them for their future lives, orthography matters very much.

> Important as creativity is, few of our charges will be professional writers in adult life, although most will be required to produce writing of some sort in connection with their work – even if it's only, say, occasional explanatory notes on an expenses claim, an accident report or an order for supplies.

We also hope that many young people will, once their inner writer is unlocked, write throughout life for pleasure, so that creative development becomes a lifelong process.

So orthography is an essential component in encouraging writing.

The challenge is to find ways of teaching orthography without stifling creativity and the fun of writing.

The following two pages contain some suggested 'dos' and 'don'ts' for supporting children in achieving accurately written creative writing.

How to achieve accurately written creative writing

Do

✓ Discuss the content of a child's writing first. That means reading for meaning and initially ignoring punctuation errors.

✓ Move on to orthography once the content is assessed, discussed and perhaps redrafted.

✓ Try to make time to look at each child's writing on a one-to-one basis. (Classroom assistants can be a great help here.) Point out the orthographical errors and get the child to correct them before making a fair copy.

✓ Maximise the use of computers for creative writing, because it's so easy to correct errors and to keep the work looking neat and professional – which does wonders for vulnerable self-esteem.

✓ Use the term 'proof-reading' and encourage children to make the concept their own too. Promote the idea that writing and proof-reading are very different, separate activities. Teach them that we can help each other (and ourselves) by proof-reading each other's work.

✓ Stress continually how important orthography is. Build it into classroom work as often as you can. Use games, quizzes, five minute fillers and reminder posters on the wall, so that the messages are constantly reinforced without making it too much of a chore.

✓ Talk to parents about this approach. Until the reasons are explained to them (emphasise that you are not sidelining the importance of spelling and punctuation), many parents are inclined to see the orthographical errors in their child's writing to the exclusion of everything else, which can make their 'help' seem very negative.

How to achieve accurately written creative writing

Don't

✗ Correct orthography when a child or student is in the process of creating a piece of writing.

✗ Comment on orthography as soon as the child shows you their work.

✗ Plaster the child's work in corrective marks in a different colour, such as red. Self-esteem is a fragile thing – especially in a child with learning difficulties or one who has become convinced by negative feedback that they are 'rubbish' at writing.

 ## Unlocking a fully literate writer

The ultimate aim, of course, is to get the child to the point where they can write creatively, with the conventions of orthography seemingly on auto-pilot.

In other words, these conventions have been so thoroughly mastered that the young writer no longer needs to think about how to spell 'necessary' or whether to put a full stop inside or outside speech marks. These things simply feed into the writing as it is composed.

 Of course, when the children are writing, this still leaves room for you – the adult – to assist with (for example) thinking of the right word for something.

When the child's first draft is complete you might:

- help with the spellings of problem words

- help with punctuation, especially upper-case letters for the beginnings of sentences and a full stop, question or exclamation mark for sentence endings, and/or

- make grammatical suggestions, especially regarding nouns and verbs.

If your own education was a long time ago, and/or if you feel less than confident about offering spelling, punctuation, grammar and vocabulary advice to children (for whatever reason), then you may find Appendix 1: *Basic Orthography* useful (it's on page 208).

Here's a fresh view from US-based teacher Teresa Ketting:

The Compact Oxford Dictionary for Students (Oxford University Press, 2006 edition) is also a useful reference book to keep handy. The main part of the dictionary is very clearly set out, with straightforward word meanings, many of which are illustrated in a single sentence. In the centre of the dictionary is an excellent section with blue-edge pages called 'Brush up your English.' It sets out the basics of grammar and punctuation in a very clear and accessible way.

'I teach first grade [equivalent to the UK's Year 1] and I encourage my first graders to use 'inventive spelling' [also known in the US as 'kid writing'] when they are writing a first draft. I think this is good because some kids get so hung up on how to spell a word that it inhibits their writing. They are learning the writing process and I encourage them to get their thoughts on paper. They know that I will be checking their papers with them for capitalization and punctuation. I am happy if they are close and they know what the word is that they mean on their paper.

'The big issues that I want my first graders to master is sentence writing and using capitalization and punctuation after each thought. I think the inventive spelling and kid *writing is something that students hopefully will outgrow as they learn more phonic skills and learn to apply them.*

I think this modelling will eventually build their confidence in their writing skills.'

 How will you punctuate this?

the policeman said the accused is lying i saw him open the safe on tuesday night

Who says that punctuation doesn't affect meaning?

 ## Using computer spellcheckers

It is very difficult to generalise about the usefulness of electronic spellchecking software.

✓ Some children insist that if they check the spelling of a word they're unsure of, then once they've seen the correct version supplied by the computer it helps them to learn it for future use.

✗ Others become so reliant on the auto-check that they seem to stop attempting to spell independently at all. Some people argue that this doesn't matter much because in adult life such writers will always be able to work at keyboards and therefore will always have access to spellcheckers.

 Schools, however, are under pressure to get these children through externally set tests and exams. Spellcheckers are not allowed in these, not even for children who have been given special needs dispensation to use a computer to write their answers.

Then there is the vexed point that some errors cannot be spotted by a spellchecker. My fingers, for example, resolutely refuse to type the word 'from'. They almost always make it 'form'. When later I run the work through the spell check for typographical errors it doesn't spot this problem ('form' is wrong, but it's not picked up because it's a valid word). So I have to go laboriously (and very carefully) though all my writing to correct this silly error manually.

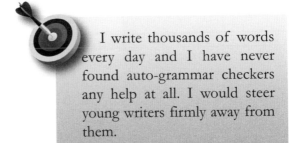

I write thousands of words every day and I have never found auto-grammar checkers any help at all. I would steer young writers firmly away from them.

The bottom line is that spellcheckers can offer a useful 'first pass' check, but they cannot be relied on and certainly must not be allowed to replace a careful reading of the text.

Creative writers can have fun too with the spellchecker's idea of what you might have meant by a badly typed word or an unrecognised proper noun. My first word processor always changed 'Shakespeare' to 'sheepshearer' and 'Vaughan' to 'vagina'. Modern ones are generally more sophisticated and fine-tuned, but I was still amused to be offered 'diamante' when I meant 'damnation' (not quite the same thing) the other day. Incidentally, smartphone 'text' spellcheckers seem to be far more aggressive in their suggestions and amendments, often with even more ridiculous results.

Encourage the children to collect these spellchecking quirks and (perhaps) weave them into a story.

It is also a way or drawing their attention to the consequences of over-reliance on the spellchecker. They must learn not to accept what it offers them without thinking.

As a final point, make sure that your device is set to the correct version of English that you use. If you are in the UK, for example, you may be lucky enough to be offered English (British) as a language to use. Failing that, go for English (International).

 In the UK you'll certainly want to avoid US English: there are many differences between UK and US spelling ('color'/'colour', 'centre' /'center', 'realise'/'realize' and so on) just waiting to confuse children who may already be finding spelling difficult.

8 And so to Orthography

Practical Teaching Ideas

Older children with specific handwriting problems

✐ Older children in Key Stages 2 or 3 who are having problems with handwriting need to be supported with some sensitivity. They may already be feeling pretty demoralised. Don't patronise them. It is important to make handwriting activities fun and satisfying for this older age group, so that they can see real improvements in their efforts.

✐ One tactic, if your own handwriting is less than perfect, is to take the line that 'We're all going to work together to improve our handwriting, because mine isn't very good either'. Or show them some 'before' and 'after' handwriting samples from a group you have worked with in the past.

✐ Handwriting schemes designed especially for this older age group are available. Some of these schemes could also help if you are working with children learning English as a second language (ESL) or as an additional language (EAL).

 If any of these children have begun their education using a language such as Chinese or Arabic, for example, they will have an especially steep learning curve.

 There is plenty of useful advice and information about handwriting on the UK's National Handwriting Association website (*www.nha-handwriting.org.uk*).

 # Making alphabet books

If you're, say, eleven (or even older) and you're still having difficulties with remembering and writing the alphabet, and with writing initial letters, you are likely be feeling pretty negative. This activity can help develop those skills, but without patronising the student.

Encourage older students who are struggling in this way to create imaginative, illustrated alphabet books – '*to help the younger children*' (of course).

These students certainly won't want anything to do with an alphabet book on their own account. But they might enjoy (and will quietly learn from) making one as a present for a five year old brother or sister, for example, or even for a local primary school Reception class.

✓ You could go down the conventional '*A for Apple, B for Bear ...*' route, or you could try to do something slightly quirkier, such as '*A for Acorn, B for Boot, C for Collar ...*' and so on.

✓ Or, for something a bit 'cooler', especially for boys, you could suggest a football team alphabet book (or series of posters): '*A for Albion, B for Bolton Wanderers, C for Chelsea ...*' etc.

 A 'geeky' child could also have fun doing this with words from new technologies too: '*A for App, B for Blackberry, C for Computer ...*' etc.

✓ Other possible themes include: TV series, characters from favourite books, people in TV soaps – or anything else you (and they) can think of which appeals.

In every case the illustrations are crucial.

✎ This activity could be undertaken collaboratively in pairs or in threes, rather than individually, if you or the students prefer. If a class or group produced several original alphabet books, you could have an exhibition and/or a competition, with an outside visitor to comment or judge.

 ## Spelling aides-memoires

✎ Old-fashioned mnemonics and other memory aids still work for some children, so it's worth collecting a variety of these and sharing them where they are useful.

necessary – one collar and two sleeves

beautiful – elephants are ugly

thorough – rough with '*tho*' in front of it

awkward – the only word in English with a pair of '*w*'s either side of a '*k*'.

✎ These can work particularly well for students with specific learning difficulties such as dyslexia.

The website *www.spelling.hemscott.net* has lots of hangman games, wordsearches, quizzes and so on designed to help parents keen to support children, adults wanting to improve their spelling and teachers needing online printable worksheets. The site is written and run by a retired English teacher.

Use all your odd moments

Two minutes at the end of the lesson? All packed up and waiting for the bell to go? Waiting to be called for assembly? Use these and any other 'odd' moments in the day to reinforce spellings.

✎ For example, choose three commonly misspelt words (such as 'disappear', 'separate', 'benefit') and call them out to be written down. Note – this is just 'spelling practice' and is definitely not a test.

Then write the words on the board yourself for pupils to check their versions against yours.

> The message of course is: *'I'm not here to show you up and I don't want to know how many you got right or wrong. But if you made a mistake with any of these, then LEARN them for tonight's homework.'*

 Or if there's time, get them to do the learning on the spot. The traditional cover and write (that is: copy the word, cover it up and write it – several times until the spelling is inter-nalised) works as well as anything for most children.

Spelling practice should always be written. Spelling aloud is much more difficult and not a particularly useful skill. In real (i.e. adult) life words have to be written down, not spelled aloud – unless you're a teacher, parent or other adult helping children.

 Another interesting way to learn spellings is to type the words into an online word cloud generator such as Wordle (*www.wordle.net*) or tagxedo (*www.tagxedo.com*). This can then be handed out to the children to learn. It's more fun than just being presented with a list of words.

Use word roots to make spelling more logical

✏ Many English words come from Latin and Greek, and even though most 21st century pupils don't get the opportunity to study these languages, they should be aware of their role in modern English.

✏ One of the ways you can do this is to refer to the origin of the word when you teach spelling. For example:

✓ 'Graphos' is the Greek word for writing. English derives lots of words from it, such as 'graphic', 'geography', 'graph', 'graphology' and so on.

✓ 'Benefit' has an 'e' after the 'n' because it comes from the Latin word 'bene' which means well (c.f. 'bien' in French).

✓ 'Dependent' uses an 'e' after the 'd' and after the 'p' because it comes from the Latin verb 'pendere' – to hang. 'Suspend' and 'pending' come from the same root.

 Anything which helps explain why a word is spelt as it is helps many children to learn and remember it.

Common error posters

✏ As a piece of creative work, ask the children to design posters for the classroom wall to show others how to avoid common errors in grammar or spelling.

Here are some common errors to get you started:

✓   when to use 'I' and when to use 'me'

✓   the troublesome question of 'laying' and 'lying', and

✓   the difference between 'to', 'too' and 'two'.

There is a list of more of these common errors in Appendix 1: *Basic Orthography*, and any grammar or spelling book will give you plenty more.

This works well on at least three levels. First, it consolidates the learning for the poster designer, who is unlikely to forget this once he or she has spent time working on the poster. Second, you end up with a resource for the classroom wall which could help other pupils. Third, display of work is, as ever, a self esteem booster.

The website *www.topmarks .co.uk* has good computer-based activities to help pupils learn grammar, spelling and punctuation.

Appendices

Appendix 1
Basic Orthography

The summary here covers most of what students need to know to inform their creative writing.

Word classes, or 'parts of speech'

 Nouns

✏ A noun is a naming word. There are several sorts.

- Common – e.g. *table, book, house, boy.*

- Proper – e.g. *Manchester, Prince William, Pizza Express, River Tyne.*

- Abstract – e.g. *adoration, anger, thirst, carelessness.*

- Collective e.g. *herd* (of cattle), *pack* (of cards), *flock* (of birds or sheep).

Verbs

A verb is the action, or 'being', word which shows you what is happening in a sentence. For example:

- We *walked* all the way to town.

- Mr Singh *is* our teacher.

- '*Run* faster' *shouted* the football coach.

- We *are* the champions.

Verbs can be expressed in various versions of the past, present and future tenses, depending on when the action or situation took place, is taking place, or will take place.

In sentences, verbs often consist of several words because they sometimes use auxiliary ('helping') verbs – *to have* or *to be* – to show the tense. For example:

- In October we *shall have been living* in our house for ten years.

- I *was wandering* along the corridor.

- You *will be* late for school.

- *Has* she *been reading* Tom's Midnight Garden?

Adjectives

Adjectives are describing words which 'qualify' or 'modify' – or tell you more about – nouns. For example:

- I love *hot, sunny summer* days.

- Drink your tea before it gets *cold*.

- *Red* roses are my *favourite* flowers.

✎ They can be used in a comparative ('more') form:

- *hotter, more exciting, better*

✎ Or a superlative ('most') form:

- *hottest, most exciting, best.*

⚙ Adverbs

✎ Adverbs are describing words which 'qualify' or 'modify' (i.e. tell you more about) verbs. They usually tell you how, when, where or why something happens. For example:

- Oliver Twist and his friends ate *hungrily*.

- My bike *rapidly* overtook hers.

- Let's do it *now*.

- Snow lay *everywhere*.

✎ Adverbs also sometimes qualify other adverbs or adjectives. For example:

- The girl was *unusually* small.

- We thought it was best to get there *quite* quickly.

- 'To die would be an *awfully* big adventure,' said Peter Pan.

Pronouns

Pronouns stand in the place of nouns. They mean you don't have to keep clumsily repeating the nouns in your sentences. There are several sorts.

- Personal (when it's the subject of the verb) – *I, he, she, we, they, it.*

  For example: '*He* and *I* went swimming.'

- Personal (when it's the object, or 'receiver', of the verb) – *him, her, us, them.*

  For example: 'Mrs Wentworth told *us* what to do.'

- Demonstrative – e.g. *This* dog, *that* pencil. Such pronouns often drop the accompanying noun.

  For example: '*This* is my idea' (rather than '*This idea* is my idea') or '*This* is mine' (rather than '*This glass/pencil/bag* is mine').

- Possessive – *his, her, hers, mine, my, their, theirs, our, ours.*

  For example: 'This is *his* book.' 'This book is *his*.' 'That is *our* house.' 'That house is *ours*.'

- Relative – *who, which, whom, whose.*

  For example: 'My cousin, *whom* you don't know, lives in Cornwall.' Or 'This is the book *which* I was telling you about.'

  In these examples the pronoun stands for 'my cousin' and 'the book'.

Prepositions

Prepositions tell you the position of something in relation to something else.

For example:

- The jam is *in* the cupboard.

- The baby is asleep *under* her blanket.

- The dish ran away *with* the spoon.

Other prepositions include: *within, inside, outside, over, beneath, above, around, up, down, into, with, at.*

But many of these words can, as so often in English, also be used to do other jobs in sentences when they are not being prepositions.

Conjunctions

Conjunctions are joining words (cf. the *junction* on a railway where two or more lines join).

They can be used to join short sentences to create longer ones, or sometimes to hook words together.

Common everyday conjunctions include: *and, or, because, as, although, but, though, so.*

For example:

- The prize went jointly to Marina *and* Oliver.

- I am going fishing at the weekend *because* it is my favourite activity. (i.e. I am going fishing at the weekend. It is my favourite activity.)

Like prepositions, conjunctions are slippery little words. The same words often get into sentences doing other jobs. Look, as ever, at *how* they are used before you decide what they are.

Articles

The is the definite article and refers to something specific.

> For example: '*the* government' or '*the* sea' refers to a specific one.

A is the indefinite article.

> For example: '*a* fox' or '*a* poem' - here it is not specific because we are referring to any fox or any poem.

An is a form of the indefinite article used when the next word begins with a vowel.

> For example: '*an* elephant', '*an* apple', '*an* old coat'.

Punctuation

This is a summary of the most important uses of the main punctuation marks used in English.

Full stops and other ways of ending a sentence

Every sentence must end with a full stop (.). Or, if appropriate, use a question mark (?) or exclamation mark (!), both of which include a full stop.

Use a question mark if a question is being asked. For example:

- How far is it to York?

- Are we nearly there?

Use an exclamation mark if you want to turn something you've written into a joke, or to make a dramatic exclamation. For example:

- Help! O my goodness!

Generally it is bad style, and very lazy, to use exclamation marks other than very occasionally. If the choice of words is strong enough, exclamation marks are usually unnecessary. You rarely you see them in newspapers, information books or in good novels (except sometimes in dialogue).

Commas

Commas are used inside sentences. Their job is to make meaning clear. They mark a natural break in the sentence or they separate one part of a sentence from another part. For example:

- Abdul, bring me your homework.

- Put that parcel over there, please.

- A tall man, Mr Smith pulled the book from the top shelf.

They are used to separate items in a list within a sentence. For example:

- Dogs, cats, guinea pigs, hamsters and rabbits all make good pets.

- I've read three books by Dickens, two by Jane Austen, two by Elizabeth Gaskell and one by Thomas Hardy.

- Excited, nervous, exhilarated and passionate, she burst through the door.

Commas are also used in pairs to separate an aside from the main thrust of the sentence. For example:

- It is unlikely, however, to happen.

- Nick Wilkins, a professor of English, told the group about studying the subject at university.

- Adela, who is new to our school, is outstanding at maths.

Capital (or upper case) letters.

Every sentence MUST begin with a capital letter.

Sometimes handwriting makes it difficult to tell whether a letter is lower or upper case (small or capital) – one of the many reasons that handwriting matters.

Most capital letters are larger than the other letters in a word – make the distinction clearly, especially when the two forms have the same, or a similar, shape – such as Cc, Ss or Kk.

Many capitals (such as Mm and Dd) are a different shape. Some, like Pp and Jj, have a different position on the page – which can lead to problems.

You also need an upper case or capital letter:

- for names (*Estella Jones, Bridgewood Preparatory School, Bristol, River Dee, Tesco* and so on). Any proper noun needs a capital letter.

- at the beginning of most lines of poetry. For example:

    Slowly, silently now the moon
    Walks the night in her silver shoon.

- for the first word inside inverted commas. For example:

    Dick said, 'And I'll come too,' when he saw us getting ready.

- for initials and acronyms (NATO, RSPCA, GCSE).

Speech marks

Also sometimes called *inverted commas* or *quotation marks*, speech marks always work in pairs. They separate a group of spoken or quoted words from the rest of the sentence.

Speech marks may be single (' and ') or double (" "). In recent years the use of single speech marks for dialogue, for example, has become more common. But both forms are still found. It is of course important that, whichever you use, you are consistent.

Note that:

- A capital letter is used each time speech marks are opened, unless the speaker is in the middle of a sentence. For example:

  'Don't you think,' continued Mary, 'that we should ask permission first?'

- A comma is usually used at the end of the spoken words inside the speech marks before the writer explains who is speaking. For example:

  'Let's go,' said James.

  'That's very interesting,' observed Latifa.

- If a full stop, question mark or exclamation mark comes at the end of a spoken sentence, it goes inside the speech marks. For example:

  'Really?' asked Alex.

  'Wow!' breathed Niamh.

- A new paragraph begins each time a different character speaks.

- If you need to use speech marks within a passage that is, in itself, in speech marks, you should use the type that you have not already used. This gives one of the following patterns:

  'Bla bla "speech" bla bla.'

  "Bla bla 'speech' bla bla."

Apostrophes

An 's' at the end of a word usually shows that it is a plural noun (e.g. *three towns*, *four dogs*, *two sticks*, etc.) or that it is part of a verb (he *says*, she *runs*, Paul *sobs*). None of these needs an apostrophe ('). So no apostrophe is needed anywhere in a sentence like this:

> All the boys in classes one, two and three enjoy basketball lessons, but Jules Atkins insists that he prefers card games.

The apostrophe has two uses. It shows:

- possession, or

- that letters have been missed out.

For possession, when the possessor is singular the apostrophe goes before the 's'. For example:

- Bernard's dog is the dog possessed by Bernard.
  (One boy – singular.)

- A term's work is the work connected with, or possessed by, the term.
  (One term – singular.)

When the possessor noun is plural the apostrophe (usually) goes after the 's'. For example:

- The girls' changing room is the changing room used, or possessed by, the girls.
  (More than one girl – plural.)

- Three years' effort is an effort lasting, or possessed by, three years.
  (More than one year – plural.)

Exactly the same rules apply to words which already end in 's' or 'ss' in their singular or plural form. For example:

- The duchess's dress (singular).

- Three actresses' autographs (plural).

- Brahms's first symphony (singular).

- Mr Watts's class (singular).

Note that plural nouns which do not end in 's' – such as *children* and *women* - behave as if they were singular and take an apostrophe before the 's' when they are possessive. For example:

- working men's club

- children's games.

The apostrophe stands in place of missing letters in contractions words such as:

- wouldn't (i.e. 'would not')

- o'clock (i.e. 'of the clock')

- shan't (i.e. 'shall not')

- C'bury (i.e. 'Canterbury' - on road signs)

- it's (i.e. 'it is' or 'it has').

Its, which means 'of it', and *it's*, which means 'it is' or 'it has', need teaching very carefully.

 # Grammar

This is a very big subject, too much to cover here. So I have highlighted just a few points which might help.

Agreement of subject and verb

✍ Every sentence has a subject. It may be one word, such as '*I ...*' or '*Katie ...*'. Or it may be something more complex, such as:

- Mr Patterson, our popular and witty Year 6 teacher ...

✍ The subject often comes at the beginning of the sentence, but this is not always the case.

✍ Not far from the subject of any sentence is a verb – the action performed by the subject. The sentence may have other things too, but a subject and a verb are the basic building bricks.

✍ It is important to make sure that your subject and verb agree. A singular subject needs a singular verb. If the subject is plural then, of course, it needs a plural verb. This is pretty straightforward in sentences such as:

- I danced.

- Katie shouted at the top of her voice.

- Mr Patterson, our popular and witty year 6 teacher, retires this year.

✍ But be careful in sentences like this:

- Ellie and Ollie *are* sister and brother.
  (The subject is 'Ellie and Ollie' – which is plural.)

- The weather, the miserable surroundings and the poor facilities *were* all responsible for our unsuccessful holiday.
  (The subject is 'The weather, the miserable surroundings and the poor facilities' – which is plural.)

- Everyone *is* here.
  (The subject is singular.)

Note that these words are all singular and need singular verbs to agree with them:

anybody	everyone
everybody	everything
nobody	either
anyone	neither
each	none

For example:

*   Neither of the men *was* guilty.
    (Singular subject.)

*   We lost several tennis balls but none *was* found.
    (Singular subject.)

*   Each of the twenty quizzes *was* harder than the one before.
    (Singular subject.)

Collective nouns are singular too:

*   The Labour Party *is* planning its next election campaign.

*   The choir *is* waiting for its conductor.

*   The pride of lions *sleeps* most of the day.

Clauses and phrases

Clauses and phrases are groups of words within sentences. A clause has a verb of its own. For example:

*   A nurse she had not seen before came and sat on the edge of her bed.

*   And I knew that one day when I was bigger I would become one of the top men.

- We were in a small room which held nothing except a large grating in the stone floor.

A clause usually adds extra detail to the main sentence, but if you remove it the sentence should still make sense. Try doing this with the examples above.

A phrase is two or more words used together in a sentence. It does not include a verb. A phrase can be a word group of almost any shape.

- We followed him through the house until we reached the kitchen.

- They had seen the film earlier that evening.

- Given the choice I like fantasy stories best.

- Simon set out wearing full climbing gear.

- Ladies and gentleman, I have an announcement to make.

Good sentences consist of varying patterns of clauses and phrases woven together.

Ten things to encourage children to remember in writing

1 'I' and 'me'

Don't confuse 'I' with 'me' when you put it with another person. 'I' is usually the subject in the sentence or clause and 'me' the object (direct or indirect).

If in doubt, leave the other person out of the sentence for a minute and work out what you would write if you were using the pronoun on its own. For example:

- Jonathan and I played cricket.
  (Think of 'I played cricket.')

- She gave him and me a telling off.
  (Think of 'She gave me a telling off.')

- Goodnight from her and me.
  (Think of 'Goodnight from me.')

- My twin sister and I are 12 years old.
  (Think of 'I am 12 years old.')

2 Himself, herself, myself

Never use *himself*, *herself* or *myself* as the subject (or part of the subject) of a sentence. For example:

- '*Sarah and myself have ...*' is always wrong.

3 Too, to and two

- I am too tall to wear these trousers.
  (Too much, or too little, of something.)

- She ate two ice creams.
  (Number.)

- May I have permission to go the school office?
  (All other uses, including part of a verb or a preposition.)

Teach this sentence to help the children remember:

- Two boys, too curious for their own good, ran to the cupboard to look inside.

4 All right

Spell *all right* correctly. It is two separate words, 'all' and 'right'. There are no such words as 'alright' and 'allright'.

But learn the difference between *all ready* and *already*. For example:

- Are we all ready to go?
  ('Ready' is an adjective telling you more about 'we'. 'All' is a separate adverb telling you more about 'ready'.)

- He has arrived already.
  ('Already' is an adverb. Here it means 'in good time'.)

5 Thank you

Remember that *thank you* is two words. So is *a lot*.

6 Less, few and fewer

Be careful with *less*, *few* and *fewer*.

- 'Less' refers to quantity.
  So you can write *less salt*, *less rainfall* and *less hope*.

- 'Fewer' or 'few' refer to number.
  So it should be *fewer eggs*, *few people*, *few schools*.

A quick way of remembering this is that if it's something you can count (e.g. eggs, people, houses) it is 'few' or 'fewer'. If you can't count whatever it is, use 'less'.

One or two British supermarkets have a notice up saying '*Baskets containing fewer than eight items*' – which is correct. Several other supermarkets get this wrong. Encourage children to watch out for it.

7 'Lie' and 'lay'

Learn that *to lie* is a verb meaning either to put oneself in a horizontal position or to tell untruths.

The past tense for the first meaning is 'lay' or 'have lain':

*   I lay on the grass all day yesterday.

*   I have lain on the grass all morning and now it's time for lunch.

On Sundays (if you're lucky) you might enjoy a lie-in – it is an error to call it anything else.

The untruth sense of *lie* is easier. The past tense is *lied* or *have lied*. For example:

*   I lied to him yesterday because I have always lied to him.

The verb *to lay* is used when the person carrying out the action (the verb's subject) is doing something to something else (i.e. when there is what is technically known as a transitive verb).

So you can *lay* eggs (if you happen to be a hen), bricks, carpets or tables. The past tense is *laid* or *have laid*, as in *new-laid eggs* or a *well-laid table*.

Remember we're dealing with three different verbs here. No wonder many children get confused!

8 'Only' in its place

It is important to put the word *only* in the correct place in a sentence. Getting it wrong (as many people do) changes the meaning.

*   Only we saw the play that afternoon.
    (No one else saw it.)

*   We saw only the play that afternoon.
    (We didn't see anything else.)

- We only saw the play that afternoon.
  (We didn't, for example, read it or rehearse it.)

- We saw the play only that afternoon.
  (We had seen it very recently.)

Take care with other adverbs such as *even*, *always* and *often*, too. 'It seemed strange even to us,' does not mean quite the same as 'It even seemed strange to us'.

9 Practice and practise

Practice (with a 'c')is a noun.

- I must do some clarinet practice.

- Practice is important if you want to improve your football.

- Dr Ahmed's medical practice covered three villages.

Sometimes it becomes an adjective:

- The practice rooms are behind the music room.

- We use the part of the lunch break as netball practice time.

Practise (with an 's') is a verb:

- I must practise the clarinet.

- Practise your football if you want to improve.

- Dr Ahmed practises in three villages.

Use *advice* and *advise* to help you remember this. They are easier because they sound different. Say aloud:

- Here is my advice (verb).

- We could try the advice centre (adjective).

- I advise you to apologise (verb).

- She advised me to come (verb).

Licence/license and *prophecy/prophesy* follow the same pattern.

 Point out that you may see this 'wrong' in American writing. In American English these words are always spelled with a 'c' even when they are verbs.

10 Writing clearly

If you use a phrase or a clause before the subject of your sentence, take care that it does not clash with the subject: For example:

- Being a wet day, I stayed indoors.
  (I am not a wet day!)

You should write:

- It was a wet day so I stayed indoors, or

- I stayed indoors because it was a wet day.

 # Spelling

There follows a checklist of the most commonly misspelt words in English, together with the words that give many children problems.

absence
accommodation
access
achieve
across
address
advantageous
aerial
analyse
anxious
arctic
argument
association
author
autumn
awkward
beautiful
beginning
benefited
biscuit
business
ceiling
changeable
commit
committed
committee
comparison
conceit
condemn
conscience
conscientious
coolly
deceive
definitely
disappear
disappoint
desirable
despair
development

dissatisfy
eerie
eligible
exaggerate
exceed
excessive
except
exhilaration
forty
fulfil
gauge
grammatical
guard
handkerchief
height
holiday
humour
humorous
immediate
independent
install
instalment
irritable
knowledge
leisure
library
likeable
lovable
maintenance
manageable
Mediterranean
miscellaneous
mischief
mischievous
necessary
necessarily
neighbour
niece
ninety

noticeable
occur
occurring
parallel
possession
proceed
procedure
profession
pursue
queue
receive
receipt
recommend
repetition
restaurant
rhyme

rhythm
ridiculous
secretary
separate
sincerely
solemn
success
thorough
truly
vicious
weird
wholly
wilfully
yacht
yield

Appendix 2

Further Reading

Unlocking the Reader in Every Child

by Susan Elkin (Ransom, 2010)

The Book Whisperer: Awakening the Inner Reader in Every Child

by Donalyn Miller (Jossey-Bass, 2009)

Children's Writers' and Artists' Yearbook

(A& C Black, published annually each August for the following year)

1001 Brilliant Writing Ideas

by Ron Shaw (David Fulton, 2007)

Teaching Creative Writing

by Graeme Harper (Continuum, 2006)

Raising Writers

by Ruth E Shagoury (Allyn & Bacon, 2008)

Index